Dancing with God Through the Storm

MYSTICISM AND MENTAL ILLNESS

Dancing with God Through the Storm

MYSTICISM AND MENTAL ILLNESS

ART AND TEXT BY

JENNIFER ELAM

WAY OPENS PRESS

MEDIA, PENNSYLVANIA

PUBLISHED BY

WAY OPENS PRESS

600 Bobbin Mill Road

Media, Pennsylvania 19063

Editorial services
and graphic design by
A Distant Wind Company
www.distantwind.com

Library of Congress Control Number: 2002104104
ISBN 0-9716525-0-3

Thank you, God,
for all of it

APPRECIATION

RESEARCHING, WRITING, and refining this book has reinforced for me the importance of our many human connections and interrelationships. We contribute in so many ways to each others' lives.

I would like to begin by expressing my most sincere thanks to the close to one hundred participants in my research project, each of whom shared their sacred stories with me, blessing me beyond measure.

Thanks also to the Cadbury Committee at Pendle Hill, who gave me the opportunity to begin this research.

Thanks to the many fine editors who helped me shepherd this book along, especially Mark William Olson, Cathleen Benberg, Rebecca Mays, Sheila Keane, and Alison Levie.

Thanks to those readers who provided much valuable input on what I was writing, especially Jeanette Reid and the large community of people who have listened to me.

Thanks to my oversight committee, which has provided me with grounding, accountability, love, and the kind of support that has held me.

Thanks to Berea Friends Meeting, especially Maureen Flannery, Harry and Laura Robie, and Dorothy Tredennick: thank you especially for traveling to Pendle Hill for the oversight meeting.

Thanks to my Pendle Hill oversight committee during the 1997–98 Cadbury year, especially Janet Shepherd, who served as clerk; Margaret Hope Bacon, who served as model; Kathryn Damiano, who served as pray-er; Rebecca Mays, who served as midwife; and Sally Palmer, who provided daily oversight of me at my computer and in the art studio, keeping me balanced in both of those creative endeavors.

Thanks to my oversight committee at Media Monthly Meeting, including Dorothy Reichardt, Louise Mullen, Esther Darlington, Sylvia Haviland, and Bernie Haviland: thank you all for supporting me and for reading this manuscript during its development.

Thanks to the staff of Special Collections at Haverford College for their support during the Gest Fellowship.

And thanks to so many others who have helped along the way, especially Chris Ravndal, who served as my teacher; Janeal Ravndal, who co-taught art with me in prison; Steve Jackson, who provided technical assistance and support; and Lloyd Guindon, who kept me grounded in trees and bird songs and who let me mow grass when I needed an extra grounding in the beauty of the physical world.

Thank you as well to all who provided my financial support: Philadelphia Yearly Meeting's Chace and Bequest Funds, the Obadiah Brown Benevolent Fund, the Lyman Fund, the Thomas H. and Mary W. Shoemaker Fund, the Elizabeth Ann Bogert Memorial Fund, the D'Olier Foundation, and the Sara Bowers Fund, as well as individual contributors.

Thank you to friends and family, who tried to understand, even when leaving my job and moving to undertake this project seemed not understandable.

Thank you to Pendle Hill in Wallingford, Pennsylvania, whose uniqueness for me lies in its provision of a relatively safe place for community moments, moments in which we can share our spiritual journeys.

Thank you to all those courageous people who live with integrity, who have modeled living in relationship with others, and who have likewise modeled community moments for me.

Thank you as well to all who value scholarship and don't hide behind it.

Thank you to all who let God's Spirit shine forth.

Thank you to all who share themselves with courage, exposing their intellect, their creativity, their inner Spirit—and the madness that haunts us all—so that we all might live our madness in ways that are less likely to do harm to ourselves or to others.

JENNIFER ELAM

CONTENTS

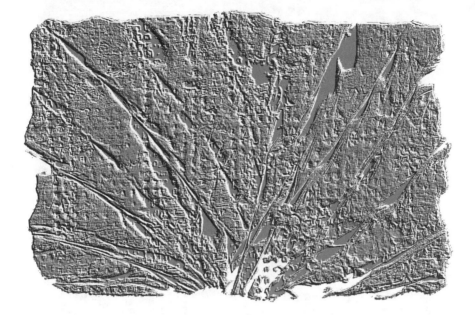

PRELUDE

"This book is an interweaving of science, intuition and art. It is likewise an interweaving of others' stories with my own ..."

Glimpsing the Blessing, Sharing the Gifts

WHILE LEADING A conference awhile back, I asked for silent worship between activities. During the worship, a participant said, "Jennifer, I'd like to see you dance your mysticism." I was stunned. Until that moment, I had never thought about "my mysticism."

I asked the group to uphold me and receive the offering in prayer. I danced. Then I led them in a body prayer, and they joined me in the dance. Sharing God with others in a dance of praise was so joyful, so right, so connected. God choreographed that moment of worship.

What was the mysticism that I danced?

I danced a connection of my physical being with the Divine. It was a prayer of praise and thanksgiving as well as a prayer of asking to be used in God's service and in God's plan. It was a surrendering of the planned program, a letting go into a Divine plan. It was an expression of praise and humility, a communion of my physical being with the Divine Being. The result was a union whose offspring was joy.

For me, mysticism involves a current of energy that connects that of God which is within me to that of God which is bigger than me. Mystical experience, as I define it, is a natural part of a committed way of living. It involves opening my soul and holding within my soul the creative space that existed before God created the universe. Mysticism opens me to a co-creation with God in that space.

The endless journey is to clear, to strip, and to clean out everything in my life that interferes with that mystical union. For me, that has included finding healing for past traumas, and it has included finding the guidance for doing so. On the mystical journey, my heart opens so that my hands can go forth and powerfully do that portion of God's work which is uniquely mine to do.

I have learned both to allow and to appreciate the gifts which are provided to me for doing this work. In my unique experience, these gifts have included images, voices, colors, Presences, languages that sing and dance, knowings, the companionship of others, rhythms that create connections, and even those separations which provide me with a glimpse of a deep pit in which I am privileged to discern opposites. Along the way, there continue to be both consolations and desolations. For each, I say "thank you" because there are gifts and lessons in them all.

For years, I practiced as a psychologist, accepting the paradigm I was taught, a paradigm that purports to identify a clear line between what is and is not mental illness. But there is no such clear line. There are only assessments or judgments made by each of us in relation to the experiences of another.

Those who participated with me in this project reported that professionals had sometimes done assessments that were helpful, assessment which had opened up their lives to greater possibilities. On the other hand, sometimes we professionals judge in ways that close off possibilities for a richer and fuller life.

I shudder to think of the potential harm that is done to others when we who are in helper roles have not dealt with our own unacknowledged fears, fears that are often triggered by those who are experiencing something that frightens us. We are sometimes quick to use labels, pathologizing another's experience in order to keep that feared experience at a distance, whether or not our actions prove helpful to the person we are "helping."

Therapists say that a large percent of their clients report experiences of God, and I believe that as a profession we have often set boundaries that have been harmful.

Perhaps something in this book will help others to see a little differently, to think a little differently—and maybe even to help a little differently.

In the course of this book, I will share a bit of the journey that led to this research, the questions I asked, the responses of my participants, and some of my own ponderings on the issues that are raised. I hope that what I have to share will prove helpful to a wide variety of readers.

Being trained as a researcher, I was naturally inclined to begin with the usual descriptive research methodologies. However, in the course of my work, I was opened to a bigger universe than the behavioral sciences traditionally embrace. So, this is not a traditional research report. It is rather a glimpse of a blessing.

In thinking about mysticism and mental illness, I conversed with close to one hundred research participants, listening to and recording their accounts. In these pages, I hope to allow some of their unique and instructive voices to be heard. Names have been changed for the sake of confidentiality, but my hope is that in listening to these otherwise authentic voices you will receive some of the same blessing that I received on first hearing them.

This book is a glimpse of the mystical. It involves an interweaving of science, intuition and art. And it is likewise an interweaving of others' stories with my own. My desire is that the different voices will flow into one another, allowing the rough edges of the integration to become more smooth.

As I listened to the personal stories of those who participated with me in this project, I was called to a role of accompaniment. People shared many different kinds of experiences. Some were quite ordinary and pleasant. Others were intense, out-of-the-ordinary experiences, even quite uncomfortable experiences. I found that to accompany those who were sharing their stories required me to maintain a level of uncertainty that is not normally valued in our culture.

Accordingly, I did not impose any set of rules for distinguishing "true" from "untrue," "authentic" from "inauthentic," that which is "of God" from that which is "not of God," or that which is "mystical" from that which is "mental illness." I found that success in the accompaniment role depended primarily on my ability to stand with individuals, neither believing nor disbelieving what they were saying. Rather, I simply tried to honor their unique experiences and allow them to make and discern their own distinctions.

In the course of my accompaniment, participants shared with me their thoughts and stories. I have included excerpts from quite a diverse collection of those accounts in this volume. As you will discover, some participants experienced no fear whatsoever as they encountered elements of a passionate, nature, or ethical mysticism.

Others did experience a degree of fear but were not overwhelmed by it. Some wrestled with God, moving through a very low time, battling depression or other difficulties for which they sought help. Still others were unable to function and were hospitalized for a major mental illness. In some cases, their experiences of God were a major part of the diagnosis.

As I reflected on these stories, I saw that there often appears to be a dance that goes on between fear and love. Afterwards, at least for many, a new life emerges, a new life of greater health, greater wholeness, greater ministry.

During the course of this project, many concerns arose in my heart. My greatest concern is that too many people, even now, are not sharing their mystical experiences. Too often, they are afraid of being labeled as "crazy." They fear that because of their mystical encounters with God, they will be perceived as having a mental illness. In some cases, even when folk need help to understand and integrate their precious experiences, they do did not seek help because the risk of having their experiences discounted in stigmatizing ways is just too great.

As a result of this study, my basic beliefs about the nature of "helping" have changed. As I grew up and as I went through graduate school, I learned many ways of "helping" through my family roles and as a psychologist. But the ways of helping through accompaniment are different, and I would not be surprised if the accompaniment model worked well with families and in psychology, too.

Accompaniment helps provide a "container" to hold those who are having unfamiliar experiences. I have embraced the task of identifying those factors which help folks who are having mystical experiences better integrate those experiences in constructive and helpful ways. I have also tried to identify those factors which can contribute to a lack of creative integration.

For the past few years, that task has involved attending to my own journey, studying the stories of saints and mystics, interviewing people having mystical experiences of God, interviewing people whose mystical encounters have contributed to a diagnosis of mental illness, and reading a broad range of relevant literature, including that of psychology and Quakerism, the religious tradition with which I identify.

Like many people in this modern age, when I began this project, I knew little about mysticism. I had never read about the lives of saints and mystics down through the ages. So I began by asking questions, trying to define and understand mysticism, trying to find some handles for even thinking about mystical experiences. The questionnaire that I developed for initial use in this research is shown in Appendix B at the back of this volume.

As my understandings grew and evolved, the response from across the country was overwhelming. I found many people hungry to talk about their experiences, eager to discuss some possible answers to the questions that I was asking.

Although this book is intended for a diverse audience, I myself am a member of the Religious Society of Friends. So I have a particular interest in helping Friends better understand the religious mystical experiences of other Friends. But I likewise hope that this book will enable people from many religious traditions to be more helpful than they have been in the past to those within their congregations or meetings who are having intense spiritual experiences.

The process of listening, of accompanying the mystical journeys of so many people, has been a transforming and enriching experience for me. I am honored by the stories that have been told, and it feels like a reverent act of ministry to share them with you in this book.

Quakers have a practice called worship sharing. In worship sharing, we are in the mode of both worship and listening on an issue or topic. When you read these stories, it is important to enter a place of both worship and deep listening, a place which is very different from getting business done as efficiently as possible. I urge you to read these stories from a personal place of worship rather than place of critique. Having this book on your desk at work to scan between business calls simply will not work.

In the course of this project, I have served in an accompaniment role as close to one hundred people recounted their stories and statements. But just as I accompanied those sharing their accounts, I hope to serve in that same role with you, the reader. I hope that you may not only enter feared territory but also leave having been as blessed and as opened as I have been.

Quakers who are well grounded in their religious heritage have the values and structures for being with people who are having the kinds of mystical experiences that can sometimes induce fear. But not everyone who has such an experience is a part of a Quaker community. And even in a Quaker meeting, more is often needed to help them integrate their experiences in creative rather than destructive ways.

So I hope that as a result of this book, the faith communities provided by churches and meetings will become more open to providing safe places for their members who are having experiences of God that they need to share. In the sharing, tremendous gifts will be released, not only for those who have been having mystical experiences but also for those who are blessed to accompany them. Such sharing, as I will show later in this book, can also release gifts for society as a whole, even serving as a powerful impetus for needed social change.

In that spirit, I invite you to join me. I invite you to join me in glimpsing a blessing.

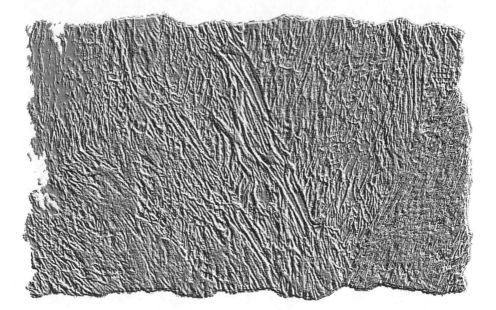

CHAPTER 1

"My methodology is that of a participant observer. This is a subject that I care about deeply . . ."

Mysticism & Mental Illness: Seeking Understandings

I BEGAN THIS RESEARCH assuming I would do it in a fairly traditional research mode. Evelyn Underhill seemed to be the most-widely accepted writer on mysticism among Quakers. So I turned to her for guidance. I intended to use Evelyn Underhill's definition of mysticism, choose qualifying participants and interview them.

Like everything else, that plan got changed. I did a pilot study at Pendle Hill, a Quaker retreat and study center. I interviewed fifteen people, asking the questions I had on my mind. The first question was "What is your definition of mysticism?" To my surprise, almost none of the answers matched Underhill's definition, and no two matched each other.

Then, for background knowledge of the classical mystics, I enrolled in a course on Christian mysticism taught by Ellen Ross at Swarthmore College. As had been the case since this project's inception, I had the sense of being exactly where I was supposed to be, even as I sat feeling intimidated by twenty-one extremely bright and very young college students. Beginning with our reading of Pseudodionysius and St. Bonaventure's version of *The Life of St. Francis,* I knew there was a relationship between what I was hearing in the classroom, what I myself had experienced, and what I was hearing from Friends across the country who were sharing their experiences with me.

The mystics, whose writings I read in my class at Swarthmore College, also offered a vast array of definitions. The kinds and stages of mysticism experienced by recognized mystics would be a fascinating study in and of itself. Although the number of stages ranged from three to thirty, most of the mystics described stages that included illumination or awareness, purgation from sin, a troubling "night," union or communion with God, and, in most cases, a return into the world to do service.

In the varied definitions by participants in this project, mysticism included the following: belief in the authority of experience beyond the ordinary senses, living experiences of oneness in all life, an awareness of truths about God, a personal experience of the Transcendent, a sense of being in the presence of Reality, the unity of all things, visual or auditory sensory experiences of a reality other than the physical world, and a loss of any sense of self or place or time. Some participants noted that mystics of all faiths and ages seem to tap into similar phenomena. Some focused on George Fox, one of the founders of Quakerism. They considered him a mystic—and Quakerism to be a mystical religion.

The more that I read and the more that I listened, the more the questions grew in my mind.

In her book, *Essentials of Mysticism,* Evelyn Underhill contends that if the word *mysticism* is used too broadly, if it is "impartially applied to the performance of mediums and the ecstasies of the saints, . . . it soon ceases to have any useful meaning." She suggests "that mysticism in its pure form is a science of ultimates, the science of union with the absolute and nothing else, and that the mystic is a person who attains to this union."

Underhill tells the story of those who throughout Western history have had this experience of unity in the actuality of their lives. She speaks of the contemplatives, the alchemists, those philosophers who have been more than theoretical philosophers, and those who have known the reality of their teachings by their own experiences before they spoke of them.

Rufus Jones in *Studies in Mystical Religion* says, "I shall use the word *mysticism* to express the type of religion which puts the emphasis on immediate awareness of relation with God, on direct and intimate consciousness of the Divine Presence. It is religion in its most acute, intense, and living stage."

He goes on to quote Howard Brinton, another respected Quaker author, saying that "all religions depend for their origin and continuance directly upon inspiration, that is to say, upon direct intercourse. The men who have made religion a living power for any people are persons who have been face to face with God, who have heard His voice and felt his Presence."

As I said, on first glance, the definitions of my research participants seemed quite different to me, but I gradually began to make sense of them as I remembered that each person is on a unique journey and at a different place on the spiritual path. That path may lead some to experience the kind of union described by Underhill. Others may experience a mystical awareness of a relationship with God as described by Jones and Brinton.

Mental illness is likewise hard to define. By its title, this book appears to be about both mysticism and mental illness, and it is. But I am not addressing all mental illness. My focus is on diagnosed and potentially diagnosed mental illness that includes experiences of God as part of the diagnosis.

I include both mysticism and mental illness in the title of the book because I found that many people with mystical experiences have fears of having their experiences discounted and of being labeled as abnormal. This book addresses both the fear that people have of being labeled and the actual labeling. I believe that part of the fear comes from the fact that people assume an absolute but mysterious standard against which experiences are assessed. They believe that failing to meet that standard will get them labeled as having a "mental illness," when, in fact, there are no absolute standards against which experiences are judged.

Even so, many people have good reasons for their fears. Sometimes, when people talk of out-of-the-ordinary experiences, friends and family members can be quick to call them "crazy." Many professionals are equally quick to diagnose mystical experiences as illness. Diagnostic assessment is a relatively subjective professional process and is very vague when it comes to experiences of God.

Most professionals use *The Diagnostic and Statistical Manual,* now in its fourth edition, as the guide for diagnosing mental disorders. The sections relevant to this research are primarily in two places. The first is Delusional Disorder, which falls under the broader category of Schizophrenia and Other Psychotic Disorders, and the second is Religious or

Spiritual Problems, which falls under the broader category of Other Conditions That May be a Focus of Clinical Attention.

The diagnostic criteria for Delusional Disorder are:

(A) Nonbizarre delusions of at least one month's duration; (B) criterion A for Schizophrenia has never been met; (C) apart from the impact of the delusion(s) or its ramifications, functioning is not markedly impaired and behavior is not obviously odd or bizarre; (D) if mood episodes have occurred concurrently with delusions, their total duration has been brief relative to the duration of the delusional periods; and (E) the disturbance is not due to the direct physiological effects of a substance or a general medical condition.

One type of delusional disorder is the Grandiose Type of Delusional Disorder. A "special relationship to a deity" is given as an example of grandiose delusion. In a description of the Grandiose Subtype, the manual states that grandiose delusions may have a religious content (for example, the person believes that he or she has a special message from a deity). It is stated that an individual's cultural or religious background should be taken into account in evaluating the possible presence of Delusional Disorder. Some cultures have widely held and culturally sanctioned beliefs that might be considered delusional in other cultures. It's recognized that the content of delusions also varies in different cultures and subcultures.

Abnormal Psychology teaches practitioners to recognize abnormality based on some combination of factors, including: 1) suffering, 2) maladaptiveness, 3) irrationality and incomprehensibility, 4) unpredictability and loss of control, 5) vividness and unconventionality, 6) observer discomfort, and 7) violation of moral or ideal standards.

These criteria for abnormality are commonly experienced when a person is called to the mystical spiritual journey. Transformations thus often occur that leave one vulnerable to being labeled "abnormal." Our world does not understand the mystical journey.

I have come to believe that each person, including each professional, has the task of determining where the boundary lies between what is acceptable in this realm of experiencing the presence of the Divine—and what is not. Problems arise when one person attempts to define that boundary for another or when attempts are made to set a boundary that is right for everyone. And, unfortunately, that is just what too many in the professional world attempt.

I believe that the boundary related to mystical experience has to be individualized. I would contend that psychiatry has often set the boundary in the wrong place for clients who have come for help. In the stories that you will read on the pages that follow, many people share their struggles with locating that boundary between what is acceptable and what is not acceptable for themselves. I respect the decisions made in each account.

While it is important for individuals to find the boundaries of acceptability for themselves, I would make one exception: in the relatively few instances when an individual perceives that he or she is being told to harm one's self or others—and acts on it—such behavior must be restrained.

Some participants have identified for themselves that they have had episodes falling on the mental illness side of their own boundary. They were in pain and sought professional help to change the experience. On either side of the boundary, pain may be present as well. Just as a mother has labor pains with birth, pain often happens with intense openings. Whether the experiences are considered as falling over one's own boundary into mental illness or merely falling into one's definition of a mystical opening into a higher consciousness, the experiences can serve to open one to a bigger and richer life, if we allow that possibility.

The subject matter of this project is critically important, even though it is often dismissed, with the people involved rather quickly marginalized.

As Rufus Jones, an eminent Quaker philosopher and student of mysticism, wrote in his book, *New Studies in Mystical Religion:*

> The mystic has a constitution which by nature is in danger of disintegration and dissociation. He is threatened with excessive centrifugal tendencies. Parts of his being incline to run off and do business on their own hook. It is essential for him, therefore, to become integrated, knit up into a coherent whole. Just that work of unification is what is usually wrought by his discovery of God. His mighty conviction tends to bind his life into a well-organized system. The divided self becomes unified. George Fox is an excellent illustration of the cohesive power of a great experience of God. It turned his darkness into light, his sadness into joy, his despair into hope, and under its influence his poor distraught mind seized upon and held to a constructive central purpose. At the same time, the whole creation seemed to him to be transfigured, "new-molded," and penetrated with a "new smell."

Seventy-five years ago, Jones was struggling with a community of people who were willing to see pathology where he believed none existed. So when there was stigma, Jones turned it around and noted that if mystical experience makes one abnormal, then he would be proud to be among the "abnormals." In fact, he redefined as abnormal anyone who did not glory in the presence of God. He described the "essential aspect of religion" as a "hushed, trembling, palpitant response of the human soul in the presence of the august, majestic, mysterious, awe-inspiring realities," which produce a consciousness of what he calls the "numinous." Jones says, "You either have it or you do not have it."

His arguments in *Mystical Religion and the Abnormal* are in response to the "New Psychologists" of his day, whom he quoted as dismissing God as a "vision of relief" and religion as a "tendency to 'project' emotional wishes into the field of reality."

Many people today wrestle with the same issues described by Jones, but they lack a frame of reference for turning around the pathological labels. Instead, some play the part of "marginalized" and know fear intimately. When a framework is available to give individuals acceptance and understanding, their religious mystical experiences are more likely to be integrated into daily life in a constructive way.

While some of the participants with whom I spoke have been helped by mental-health professionals, others believe that their mystical experiences were mislabeled as mental illness, leading to ineffective or inappropriate treatment by professionals. For example, the woman that I call Susan was hospitalized against her will. A non-Quaker psychiatrist diagnosed her primary symptoms as "grandiose delusions." The same expression of religious belief was described as "sincere seeking of the Light" by a Quaker psychiatrist and by her Friends meeting. Eventually, her monthly meeting successfully petitioned for her release.

The need to look at the relationship of mysticism and mental illness is well-documented. In *New Studies in Mystical Religion,* published in 1927, Rufus Jones laments that "New Psychologists . . . have leaped to the conclusion that religion is a mild form of mental disease." Similarly, in Pendle Hill Pamphlet 104, entitled *Psychoanalysis and Religious Mysticism* (1959), David McClelland discusses the taboo among psychologists toward having any religious commitments and the unacceptability of talking about religious mystical experiences. Unfortunately, this tendency to discount spiritual experiences is still present today.

In her article "Mental Illness and Spiritual Crises," Judith Miller points out that sometimes experiences presently being labeled psychotic are leading to positive, growth-producing outcomes. Similarly, in his article, "Inner Voices: Distinguishing Transcendent and Pathological Characteristics," Mitchell Liester says, "Despite our culture's ego-retentive tendency to view intuitive and revelatory inner voices as 'unreal,' or even worse as symptoms of pathology, these voices are a powerful, influential force in our world."

In a book published by the American Psychological Association in 1996, editor Edward Shafranske points out that psychology is still struggling with how to view religious experience in framing and treating mental illness.

Faith communities that value and embrace the mystical life and see mystical experiences as real and valid have much to offer. Through their openness and inquisitiveness, such communities can invite people to talk of their experiences, knowing that they will be valued. Such a environment, rather than an assumption of pathology, allows those who have unusual experiences of God to feel safe in sharing their stories.

For the sake of any academics who may be reading this book, I should acknowledge that the methodologies used in this project are exploratory in nature and the population sample was not random. That means that when statements are made in this book, they generalize only to these participants and not to broader communities.

With that disclaimer in place, let me say, however, that I think that many of the statements made *could* apply to broader communities, though obviously further research is needed.

My methodology is that of a participant observer, which is to say, I am not just studying the subject as an academic pursuit, and I do not claim the role of objective observer. This is a subject that I care about deeply. It has significance in my own life.

I am not the first to travel this path. Two Quaker psychologists, Barbara Owen and Susan Ziechner, have courageously used participant observation methodologies in their dissertation research on transcendent experiences. They provide great models of how helpful the information gathered through these methodologies can be. They correctly assumed that participants were capable of being co-researchers and that exploration of personal transcendent experiences would contribute to the body of research in their profession.

I also assume that valuable information can be gathered when participants are allowed to decide whether or not their experiences are "mystical." I found that throughout history mysticism has been defined in many different ways, and this sample of participants reflects some of that variety.

I chose not to include many fields of study that overlap with my own: mysticism of religious traditions other than Christianity, near-death experiences, drug-experience research, psychic phenomena, dream interpretation, and many others.

I have chosen to limit this study to Christian mysticism and to include only those experiences determined by the participants to be mystical. My sample does not include people having experiences of God in which they believe God is telling them to harm themselves or others. I make the assumption that those behaviors must be curtailed, independent of discernment of whose voice they are hearing.

To obtain participants, notices were placed in *Friends Journal, Friends Bulletin, What Canst Thou Say* (a newsletter for Quaker mystics), the Pendle Hill quarterly bulletin, and on the Pendle Hill web page. Obviously the voices that I heard were primarily Quaker in origin, but I believe that the lessons learned and the insights shared have significance beyond the Quaker world.

The major purpose of this book is to provide a place for souls and spirits to connect with each other. As we read one another's sacred stories in the spirit of worship, as we retain the pulse and heartbeat of those stories, we find connection replacing alienation. It is my intent to share this material in a manner that will convey the respect and admiration that I have for all courageous souls living their spiritual journeys of faith in such special ways.

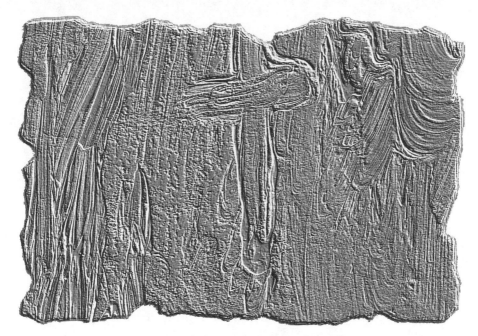

CHAPTER 2

"I saw the same
grey-white homespun
woolen robe next to
me and felt the
warmth of someone
who had been walking
in the sun . . ."

Mysticism as a Verb: Classical Expressions

THE CLASSICAL LITERATURE on mysticism tends to focus on three major kinds: passionate mysticism, nature mysticism, and ethical mysticism. Experiences fitting into each of these three types were present in some of the stories that I heard while undertaking this project.

Like other kinds of mystical experiences, the classical expressions of passionate, nature, and ethical mysticism tend to transform those who experience them, often leading individuals in new directions.

Those who participated with me in this research seldom reported experiences that would fit any of the classical categories purely or exclusively. Sometimes, for example, they reported experiences of more than one kind. Other times, their mysticism was intermingled with other experiences that don't fit the classical categories at all.

Before considering a wider range of mystical experiences, it's important to have a sense of the classical categories and how they sometimes find expression in a contemporary context.

PASSIONATE MYSTICISM includes those experiences of communion or union with God that involve a deeply personal experience of what is often referred to as Christ's "passion," especially his crucifixion or resurrection.

Julian of Norwich is an example of a passionate mystic. Her fourteenth-century visions featured many variations on Jesus' crucifixion at the hands of the Romans. She was devoted to a life of prayer and contemplation. And through that prayer and contemplation, she was given sixteen "showings" in which God spoke to her. She spent the rest of her life living out what God had shown her.

One of her beliefs, which contrasted with the religion of her times, was that the body is good. Julian had numerous unusual visions of the body of Christ. In one, for example, she saw Jesus as having not a wound in his side but a womb.

Howard Brinton, a Quaker writer, describes NATURE MYSTICISM in a 1967 book as "the concept of nature as a spiritual reality rather than as a purely physical one." He calls it "the oldest mysticism recorded."

In St. Bonaventure's classic *The Life of St. Francis,* there are many examples of Francis's mystical connections with animals and the natural creations of God. Over the centuries, these stories have endeared him to the hearts of many. Similarly, George Fox the founder of Quakerism, is said to have found during one of his mystical experiences that "all creation had a new smell."

Through nature mysticism, the created world often takes on new meaning and new freshness. While in meeting for worship, mystical messages might come involving a transforming experience of nature. A deepened reverence for God's creation and a deeper connection with our own creation energy is also common.

ETHICAL MYSTICISM refers to the practical or ethical application of faith as an intentional result of the mystical experience.

In Pendle Hill Pamphlet #156, *Ethical Mysticism in the Society of Friends* (1967), Howard Brinton described ethical mysticism as an important part of Quakerism. "By ethical mysticism," he writes, "I mean that type of mysticism which first withdraws from the world revealed by the senses to the inward Divine Source of Light, Truth, and Power, and then returns to the world with strength renewed, insight cleared, and desire quickened to bind all life together in the bonds of Love. These bonds are discovered by the process of withdrawal and return because the one inward Divine Source is itself the creative unity which seeks to bind all life together."

Many of the contacts that I used during this project were made through Quaker circles, and many of the stories I heard included mention of the importance of performing God's work. Perhaps that's because it's not uncommon for Quakers to feel called to service as activists, social-service providers, teachers, or other beneficial professions. In keeping with the values of ethical mysticism, many who shared their stories with me felt that they were serving God through their work.

The following excerpts, taken from participants' personal stories, illustrate some of the ways in which the three classic forms of mysticism sometimes find expression.

ASKING JESUS TO JOIN ME ON THE FACING BENCH
Robert's story, an example of passionate mysticism

I surrendered my will to God in meeting for worship and had a vision of gray-white robed hands coming down and resting on my shoulders.

In a subsequent experience, after asking Jesus to join me on the "facing bench" at meeting, I saw the same gray-white homespun woolen robe next to me and felt the warmth of someone who had been walking in the sun. I felt the touch of the hands and entered a new level of stillness that did not end with the rise of meeting. Two years later, the stillness is still available to me.

I have had other visions and awarenesses, but nothing else as profound or transforming.

I could talk about these experiences with others and never felt as though I was going crazy. I was fearful for a moment, but that passed as I became accustomed to the new stillness. I spoke about it to people who I felt would understand, people of spiritual experience and depth. Those who understood affirmed and companioned my experience; those who didn't understand simply tolerated or dismissed it.

My life has been changed by this experience. People tell me that I am calmer, a peaceful presence in a world accustomed to chaos. I am also less assertive and outwardly goal-oriented than I was in the past. Once a planner, now I have no plans, much to my wife's consternation.

I used to care about how much money I made. I'm still concerned about how bills will be paid, but I am not as able to do anything about it. My purpose in life has changed from improving the City of Man to upholding and bringing forth the City of God.

I look for an edge of reality, a grounding for the fantastic. For me, mysticism is a belief in the authority of experience: experience that goes beyond the ordinary senses. I am suspicious of any mysticism which disdains the affairs of daily life.

Robert's story illustrates aspects of passionate mysticism. His search for peace in life took him to a vision of Jesus joining him in worship at a Quaker meeting. As is often the case with this and other forms of mysticism, his vision facilitated a personal transformation. There was a resurrection of stillness in his life that has stayed with him, guiding his daily activities.

WHEN JESUS CAME INTO THE ROOM
Howard's story, an example of passionate mysticism

Several years ago, when I was going through a painful struggle related to ministry efforts of a difficult nature, I was feeling burned out and abandoned by God. At a retreat with "Friends in the Spirit of Christ," I explained my situation and asked Friends present to pray for me. They put me in a chair in the middle of the room and gathered around me with some laying on of hands.

In the midst of the prayer, I experienced Jesus present in the room, imploring me to let loose of the pain, anger, and frustration and allow him to take these things upon himself, as he did long ago on the cross. I was not meant to carry this stuff around with me. It had only become an opportunity for the evil one to get me to focus on my wounds and victim status instead of my healing.

In Jesus' presence, I felt my body relax and my wounds being taken from me. There have been times since then when I have slipped back into the same tendency to focus on my woundedness and anger. Remembering this experience has always helped me catch myself and remember my healing and resurrection.

I have felt comfortable telling this experience. I don't tell everyone I know, but if I perceive the person to be religious and/or the issues of darkness and pain come up, I will share if the occasion seems right.

I have received nothing but positive feedback during the times that I have shared this experience. I'm sure there have been people that are a bit weirded out by it, but they have never communicated anything but warm acceptance. I would not share with secular types who I feel would not understand my experiences.

My biggest struggle is in continuing to integrate this experience into my life. I still have a weakness for anger, especially a tendency to focus on my "self-righteous" anger, attributing it to God.

For Quakers and people of other prophetic religious traditions, it is very tempting to believe that one's anger at some injustice is really a prophetic word from God, speaking truth to power. But I have found, mostly through pain, that ministry given from this spirit usually has negative fruit both for those who receive it and for me in particular. It leads into a denial of the healing power of God.

My definition of mysticism is direct and personal communication with the living God. And my mystical experiences have generally been of the type in which God calls me to focus on my healing, not my wounds and anger. Again, I don't always focus very well, but the continual reminder and more disciplined practices of prayer, study, and fellowship have helped remind me of the validity of my mystical experiences and urged me to trust in these and continue to seek integration.

Howard connects with the crucifixion by asking God, "Why hast thou forsaken me?" From there, he moves into the healing power provided by Christ's willingness to take our beatings on his back. By his stripes, we are healed, says the Scriptures.

When Howard accepts the invitation to let Jesus take the pain, he is able to let go. Like many of us, Howard sometimes gives it up and then takes it back. But his knowledge of the option to let it go is clear, made real with a specific vision of Jesus' presence and invitation.

MYSTICISM AS A VERB
Liesel's story, an example of passionate mysticism

I define mysticism as a relationship with God; it's how you relate to God. Your growing relationship with God is constantly evolving. The word *faith* comes to mind, *faith* as a verb. Mysticism and faith are connected. Mysticism is also a verb because it involves a constantly moving relationship with God.

It is totally new for me to think that I could have a mystical leading like George Fox, the founder of the Religious Society of Friends, had. But I have been moved by John 1:13, which says that I was born out of God. And I have had experiences this year that have me recognizing my origin, my point of being.

Once, when I was feeling lousy, I let myself go with that feeling. I was wrapped in an awful feeling. My Bible was on the bookshelf. I opened it to 1 Corinthians, to Paul's teachings on love. I read it and repeated it to memorize it.

"Love is kind..." I internalized it. It was talking about God, and

I realized over and over my connection. I have had that same experience of connection two or three times recently.

John 15:5 says, "Without me, you can do nothing." That phrase implies intimacy. I used to think of God as "out there." Now I am in God, and God is in me. The word mysticism is still "out there," but it is getting into me. My experiences fit my definition.

Another time—well, I have been reluctant to talk about this one, a little fearful. But one day I was down at the beach doing centering prayer. I swam about a quarter of a mile. I closed my eyes. I love to be outside, feeling the water and the wind. Wind in Greek is Spirit, as in breath. I had the feeling of being wrapped in the Spirit. Then I had the sense I was reliving Jesus' crucifixion when I was dealing with something that upset me. On the cross, he was realigning himself with God. And I felt as if I was working on realignment as I worked on this issue.

A cloud came over the sun. It got darker and cooler. I saw my footprints disappearing in the sand. I didn't see anything but sensed a presence. I felt I was in the tomb with Mary Magdalene. There was a scene in John where Jesus said, "You must let me go so I can live within you." I wasn't letting go so that this person could live within me. The experience has stayed with me.

The idea of calling myself a mystic is a new concept. I am becoming more aware of this word mystic. Using my definition, I am evolving into a mystic. I am becoming a person who is in communion with God and who is inviting God in more and more. I am leery of saying I am a mystic. I would rather say that I am a child of God.

How I relate to people mirrors how I relate to God. Like on the beach, I wasn't letting go of Jesus. I was having problems with letting go. It seems that the way I live my life and my spiritual life are intertwined.

My work with clay mirrors my relationship with God. The word "pruning" is important. John talks about how God is the vine and we are the branches. In Greek, the word prune means to cleanse. When I build a pot, scraping is the action of pruning or cleansing. God prunes me as I prune the pot I am making. I am scraping away layers that keep me from God.

I have been told I am "exercising my God muscle," and I am wanting to. We have the capacity to be more like Jesus. "Live up to the light and more will be given," says Caroline Fox in London Yearly Meeting's Faith and Practice. I want to be more open, more trusting, more mystical. Still, I don't know about calling myself a mystic. My experience compared to others is different.

The first person I told about my experiences was my cousin. My cousin is Catholic, and Jesus and Christ are central. I had a need to share, but I wasn't going to share with someone who would laugh at me. Then I told my dad. It is an intimate thing; this is delving into an intimate area of life. I felt vulnerable. How could I reveal something so close to me?

I knew I wasn't crazy because I have a good sense of myself. It wasn't a vision or anything, just a sense of Jesus' presence and a sense of my being in the tomb.

Sharing keeps the experiences alive. The flame burns brighter when it is shared. I wanted to have a burning heart and be a disciple on the road to Emmaus. Sharing also brings us closer. I want to be as close to my parents as possible.

God is alive to my father as part of his daily life. He is Christocentric. Christ and Jesus are central figures in his life. We are alike in many ways. I knew he would understand and appreciate what I had said. He'd understand the significance.

Liesel speaks of the vulnerability that was part of the spiritual journey, both for Jesus and for her. It seems we get to our truest strength by going through this vulnerability with faith. As she says, there is often a need to share, and much discernment is needed about whom to share with and when. There is a deep need to know and be known, as well as to be understood and accepted. Yet it is unclear at times where that can be found.

Liesel connects with John's words, "Now, I am in God and God is in me," and she connects with Paul's words on love. The connection is not just intellectual: it is living those words and becoming one with what the words represent. There is a passion that comes alive in making such connections.

YOUR LIFE IS FINE
Tom's story, an example of nature mysticism

For me, mystical experience means feeling strongly the presence of God. And this has happened a few times for me.

For instance, I once went on a trip that involved a long period of being out in nature by myself. I had been looking for bald eagles. I heard where they were to be, but it was very cold. With binoculars I was looking across the water at snow patches. Methodically, I would go up each tree, putting all my attention into watching.

In the course of this, the world opened up.

It was a bright, sunny, windy winter day. My senses were heightened with the feel of the wind, the reflection of the water, and the smell of the salt marsh. I had an acute sense of being a part of everything.

I didn't see an eagle. What I felt had to do with the looking, the preparedness, the waiting, and the desire to see. Years later, people remembered hearing me speak about looking for eagles. It struck them and me. It was an instant that didn't last long, but it was beyond time. It was endless.

I had the same experience in nature while paddling my kayak in Chesapeake Bay, a sense of a unifying mystical experience, just part of everything, beyond thinking. If I think about it, I lose it.

Last year in the Grand Canyon I saw a blue sky with puffy cumulus clouds. I looked across the meadow at the pines and aspen trees—and tears came.

I found myself sobbing. Yet from nowhere, I felt this sense of love and acceptance from God saying, "Your life is fine." The details are inconsequential because God was saying that it's all fine. I couldn't be bothered by career, relationships, or anything else.

When I told other people about this, some knew the exact place where it happened. Four or five people I know have been brought to tears in that same spot. Other people, when you tell them, look at you like you're crazy.

On my last vacation, I wanted this same peak or mystical experience, but it didn't happen. Those experiences are gifts of grace that don't happen when I try to achieve them. It is when I follow what I deeply feel I am supposed to be doing that they are more likely to happen.

When I am around Bill Taber [a teacher and leader among Quakers], I sometimes sense a presence available in the room. Some people just speak with an authority, a bodily felt knowing. I associate that with the mystical. It is a knowing in the body, beyond the head.

Sometimes I think about what it's like in the desert looking at stars, an upside down bowl of stars. I told my cousin that, and she thought I was crazy. I was so taken aback. It was so special for me, and she didn't get it at all. This Christmas, she took a trip on the Amazon and talked about looking at the stars. She apologized to me; now she knows.

When I share with others, one of the most helpful things is the knowing in their expression. I know if they have experienced something because they can put the experience into a framework or words that "speak to my condition." The one who can best speak to you is the one who has been through the event. They can empathize and identify in a believable way. Often the responses are nonverbal, tone of voice or body language.

It's clear that God's gifts in the natural world provide Tom the spiritual connection that energizes him for the harder parts of his life. As a result, he has clear ideas of what works in his life and what does not.

A GIFT OF PEACE: QUESTIONED, TESTED
Dick's story, an example of both nature and ethical mysticism

I grew up on small farms in Iowa during the depression. Mother took my older brother and sister and left Dad and me. I was nurtured by various adults—and especially by nature. As an adult, I love and feel most secure, whole, and connected to all when among nature.

My adolescence was painful, and I was sent to a Quaker boarding high school where I began to try to find deeper and wider meaning in my life.

Deeply troubled while trying to determine if I should break with my mother's family's tradition of military service, I had the first of my rare, but for me, important experiences of peace and connectedness.

Gazing at a wooded scene, the plants seemed to become lighter and perhaps even to shimmer in the light a little, as if an energy behind them was throbbing. I felt connected to the universe. My feelings were profound but probably only lasted a few seconds or even possibly a few split seconds. Then a wave of deep peace began to well up within me, as if from my center, filling me with a peace I had not experienced before.

I took it for a sign that I was to object to war and become a conscientious objector, which was the decision I had been moving toward while feeling conflicted. Thereafter, I went forward to become a conscientious objector and never felt any deep leadings to change my course, though intellectually I repeatedly questioned my motives and actions.

I have had only a few such experiences in my life. But those brief experiences have provided the essential direction and inspiration for my lifelong spiritual journey and for my becoming a social worker.

It was true that I had been reading a book about mystics, so this undoubtedly influenced me, or at least helped me be more open to the experience. I don't consider such experiences to have been especially mystical. There were no voices or visions or powerful emotions. The result was mainly peace, with a muted but deep joy. Such experiences are grounded in nature, where I feel most comfortable and connected.

Perhaps by grace, the Holy Spirit comes to me when I am most troubled. That grace seems to come to me most often when my nervous system is high-strung, prone to depression, anger, frustration, or excitement. Probably I would be burned up by any stronger currents of spirituality. Or maybe I would "go off the deep end."

The peace I receive has been just enough to help me with key decisions. It comes during periods of loss and grief or depression and frustration. It gives me courage, inspiration, and hope, just enough to keep me going.

Other than those few, brief, blessed moments, which I can never forget, I occasionally have brief experiences of bliss and joy and assurances, sometimes in meeting for worship, sometimes alone in nature, and sometimes at odd, unexpected times. These have been rare but important for me. I take them as a sign to keep up hope and keep keeping on, a sign to help me gather more courage.

I emphasize that these experiences are not spectacular. I love nature, and when I gaze at a lovely scene in nature, I am already close to the Creator.

Sometimes while I am in Friends meetings, I am "there," or almost "there," but even this occurs rarely. Gradually, my meeting and prayer experiences are becoming more meaningful more often. I hope to come closer to Brother Lawrence's example, when work and life itself can become a prayer to and with God, as constantly as possible.

I am definitely a weak and needy person. But this apparent "curse" may be, as Marti Matthews, the author of *The Gift of Pain*, suggests, a blessing spiritually.

Because I am weak, I need grace, I need the Holy Spirit, I need God. Difficult experiences in my life keep reminding me of my needs. These weaknesses, problems, troubles, depressions, confusions, and so forth, seem to remind me of my need for grace, even when I forget, even when I get busy, even when I rush off in my own pig-headed projects and directions. I have plenty to remind me of my need for grace.

Probably it is need that drives my spiritual life, not great experiences or insights produced in blinding light. But I greatly treasure my few brief and "moderate" experiences of grace, which I consider divine gifts and leadings.

If anyone wished to argue that my feeling of peace stemmed from need, despair, or wishful thinking, that perhaps I only imagined or hallucinated seeing some "extra" light or lightness in nature, I wouldn't bother to argue with that interpretation. Why would I? My relationship with Jesus and what is called the Holy Ghost or the Spirit of Truth or the Inner Light blesses me with a rational mind, but that same relationship also allows me to accept and live with paradoxes, uncertainty, doubts, and contradictions. I believe Jesus, even in his recorded teachings, also respected paradoxes.

What I do know is that for a very brief moment, I felt a deep feeling of peace welling up from within me—a stronger sense of peace than I have felt at any other time.

The test? "By their fruits ye shall know them."

The few experiences I have described have given me direction, hope, peace, inspiration, and courage. When I have acted on these apparent "leadings," the results, even if gained through difficulty, pain, turmoil, and recurring doubt, have proved to be in accordance with the teachings of Jesus and of the greatest humanistic philosophers. In concrete worldly terms, they have helped bring about more just and humane relationships and conditions. So I believe that the effects of following these "leadings" have stood the test of time.

Now if only I can move closer to Brother Lawrence's example of practicing the presence of God, in all of my life, so that I might "pray without ceasing…"

Like most of us, Dick has moments of deep gratitude for the spiritual gifts in his life. At other moments, his rational mind can question, acknowledge, and even affirm the possibility of other interpretations of these gifts.

Dick's story includes elements of both nature mysticism and ethical mysticism. He shares with us how his conviction toward conscientious objection came directly from a spiritual opening in a wooded setting. As the plants around him took on an unusual lightness, a peace welled up within him. The "cause for war" was taken away.

Dick accepts the spiritual gifts he has been given. He knows as well that the rational mind is a gift from God. So he lives with—and sometimes struggles with—the seeming contradictions. Dick knows the truth of both parts of himself and does not have to choose between them. In like manner, he has developed a test for the "leadings" he has experienced, a test that serves to validate the paradoxes of his life. What gifts!

JESUS BECAME MY INWARD FRIEND
Marshall's story, an example of both ethical and passionate mysticism

For me, mysticism is simply a name that has been given to that direct invasion of our feelings by the divine Presence. I believe that we all possess an inner faculty to respond to this direct invasion, which leads to a greater knowing of the spiritual world.

What happens is beyond words. It is experiential, ineffable. It is not extrasensory perception, and it should not be associated with occult experiences. It is not confined to special temperaments. It is not an escape from the realities of this everyday world.

Sometimes it is very individual. But it can also be a group experience, such as might happened during a Quaker meeting for worship based on silent waiting and obedience.

Jesus was a Jewish mystic, and it seems to me that the early Christian experience was a mystical one, an experiencing of the Inward Christ. Those who have experienced a "gathered meeting" for worship know the power of that experience, which is mystical. The prophets of the Old Testament experienced a direct inner message from God. Just as we have a faculty for reason, we all have a mystical faculty. Many, I would suppose, have mystical experiences and simply don't name them as such.

A mystical experience can be transforming. It can change one's life. It is a fleeting experience, but a knowledge-giving experience. I believe it grows out of an inward faculty that can be cultivated by spiritual disciplines—regular attendance at a Friends meeting for worship, for example—or by awareness of being on a spiritual journey. It is a faculty within that can be alive for a lifetime if we obey the inward nudges. There is the universal inward potential in everyone, and there is the experience itself.

Personally, I have felt the power of a gathered meeting for worship, a meeting where we were all "one in the Life."

The meeting that first comes to mind occurred in Kenya. It was at a Friends World Committee for Consultation gathering. A large group of Friends from all continents of the world, with various backgrounds and with a diversity of faith and practice, knew to the core of their being, in the experience of waiting worship, that they were "one" in spirit. Theological differences melted away. It is beyond words to articulate the melting down, the power of that Presence.

On a personal level, when I was an intern teacher at a Friends school, facing the prospect of contacting my draft board, I struggled to find a direction. I was divided in mind and spirit, not sleeping nights. I felt alone in the midst of friends. Few were aware of my inward struggles. I even felt my loving parents would not understand. This lasted for weeks until I could at last know an indescribable wholeness and inner peace. That wholeness and peace grew in me day by day. I felt in touch with the world around me in a fresh and energy-giving way.

The Scripture readings I had been doing began to illuminate my consciousness. The words of John Woolman had a similar effect. I knew I was beginning a spiritual journey not unlike Woolman's in nature yet in a different measure. Woolman became my friend. Jesus became my friend. They became my inner companions. I was no longer alone.

I can still recall the physical effect on my person. There were fleeting moments of inner joy. At the time, my only outlet was to share passages from Scripture and from Woolman with students and teachers. This could be done publicly during readings at breakfast time. Meetings for worship at the school took on a new character.

It followed, of course, that I faced my draft board and became a conscientious objector. I now look back upon this illumined experience as an opening in my life that set a course for a lifetime. It was not an intellectual experience. It was an ethical mystical experience.

Since that time, I have read the journals of several Friends and realize that what I was experiencing then has also been experienced by others. I found in my heart a gospel of good news. Yes, Jesus was present, an inward companion. New friendships were born.

Mysticism is not a retreat from the world. It is the other side of action in the world. All this is in the Christian context, but it is inclusive. I came to it through Christ.

Over the years, I have stumbled and betrayed my Inner Guide. But even as I stumble, I know at the same instant what will pick me up and set me on course. During the war, when I was serving with other C.O.s in a New Jersey state institution, it was my assignment to meet with the superintendent of the institution who had a son in the U.S. Air Force in the South Pacific. These were very soul-wrenching occasions, and I was often close to despair.

I shall not forget a weekend silent retreat in northern New Jersey, sponsored by Pendle Hill. It was my first experience at a silent weekend. It was silent except for two presentations by the retreat leader. This silence was a soothing poultice for my soul. I cannot recall words that were spoken in the presentations. I cannot recall quotations in the readings I found in the library. But I do recall what happened in the silence.

I returned to my job at the state institution with renewed patience for my superior. I experienced love for him, realizing the pain he must be in. I would now say this was a measure of what others have experienced to a greater degree. But the experience in itself is the same, and I believe it happens to many of us in all walks of life, both here and in other cultures.

The experience, I now know, takes on new dimensions if we are obedient. We stumble, but inwardly we know the cure: putting oneself in the presence of God each day.

I have heard others in the Friends community speak of their spiritual experiences. I have traveled among very diverse groups of Quakers, including those labeled "evangelical," "liberal," or "conservative." Some of the experiences that they have shared appear to me more helpful than others. The ones which have been most helpful are ones where I immediately felt a sense of integrity: the more unpolished, perhaps the better.

It is of great help if one has known the person over a period of time. In some situations, one knows immediately where words are coming from when spoken by a complete stranger.

I cannot explain this inner faculty that we all possess, but as we travel on in the spiritual quest, regardless of our outer profession or work, we come to that place where we know what is in "the Life" and what is not in "the Life." One's spiritual community can often better discern this than can an individual. So if one is part of a spiritual community, the gift will be more widely shared.

Many Quakers live the kind of ethical mysticism that Marshall describes. As a result of their spiritual experiences, and as a practical application of their faith, they feel divinely called to service.

Isaiah says, "They that wait upon the Lord shall renew their strength." Many describe a transformation and renewed strength following mystical experiences. Most Quakers believe it is important to return to the world after a period of withdrawal; they believe that their renewed strength can be used for positive action in the world.

Perhaps the most loved story among contemporary Quakers is John Woolman's spiritual commitment to support the abolition of slavery, even when many fellow Quakers did not understand his calling.

Woolman's call to service was about living his faith with integrity. And the strength that he was given to pursue that calling serves as a reminder. It is a reminder for many that reverence for life is an inherent and natural part not only of ethical mysticism but of passionate and nature mysticism as well.

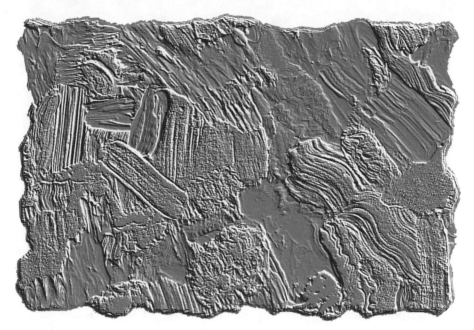

CHAPTER 3

*"I was experiencing a
duality, a place where
opposites meet and
mean the same thing,
like seeing both sides
of a mirror . . ."*

*Common Journeys,
Diverging Paths*

A S I BEGAN this project, I asked questions of everyone I knew. I wanted clarity. I sought definitions.

One of my first priorities was to discern the difference between mysticism and mental illness. Assuming a sharp distinction between the two, I wanted to learn where and how to draw the line.

Perhaps I was unduly influenced in this by some of the people I spoke with. They suggested to me that there is a fine line between mysticism and mental illness and that it would be valuable to be able to discern the difference between the two. Being trained in psychology myself, I readily accepted that view.

As a result, the model with which I began this study looked somewhat like two circles with a clear and impenetrable line between the two (figure 1, next page). On one side was mental illness; and on the other, mystical encounters with God.

But before long, I discovered that the questions that one asks can sometimes reveal much about one's biases and one's ignorance. And

with the help of some of my participants, I began to recognize the threat to
the dignity of others inherent in my
questions.

In our culture, mental illness carries
a stigma, a stigma that effectively mar-
ginalizes those so labeled. More often
than not, the insights, gifts, and contri-

FIGURE 1

Two circles, a clear line between

butions of those who are called mentally ill are simply discounted.
Sometimes those contributions are even treated as "symptoms."

So in exploring the boundary between mysticism and mental illness, I was treading on dangerous ground. For example, what does it
do to the soul of another human being to suggest that his or her experiences of God might be "inauthentic," "false," or even "delusional?"

It seemed, through my questions, that I was inadvertently forcing
others to choose between two unacceptable alternatives. On the one
hand, they could deny their experiences and their soul's center—and
thereby accommodate the demands of a society which tends to believe
that most intense God experiences are "false."

Or, on the other hand, they could talk about their experiences and
get stuck with the label "crazy" or "mentally ill," accepting all the negative ramifications such labels imply.

I began to wonder: *When there is a conflict between the demands of
our society and our own experience, who do we honor—and at what cost?*

Eventually, I realized that it's irresponsible to force anyone into
making such choices, for such choices in and of themselves are "crazy-
making." I am indebted to all who helped make this clear to me.

When I revised my line of questioning to focus on the relationship
between mysticism and mental illness, rather than on the boundary
between the two, every conversation became more fruitful.

As I listened to stories with this line of questioning, and as I pondered the nature of my own experiences, it seemed less like two separate worlds with a sharp line between them. In fact, it seemed much
more like a set of deeply overlapping circles (figure 2, next page). In
fact, the more I listened, the more overlap I heard.

One woman's reaction to all of this was especially intriguing to me,
and I want to share with you her story.

When I first spoke with Helene, she was nineteen. She was bright
and articulate. Here was a woman who had been hospitalized for what
had been called a psychotic break—and who had had experiences that
she considered mystical.

Helene is the only person I have ever talked with about being put

FIGURE 2
Two circles, progressively more overlapping

in a mental hospital who appears to have almost no shame around her hospitalization. Perhaps because of the very intentional ways in which her mother and community supported her, she hasn't let the experience marginalize her or leave her with a sense of disgrace.

At last report, Helene was living with her parents and working in a preschool. She had plans to study Reiki (the pursuit of a higher spiritual consciousness through the application of "universal life force energy") and other healing arts.

I interviewed her just three months after her hospitalization. She described her experiences as a "psychotic break." But in the course of our conversation, Helene also talked about the beauty of being opened to mysteries of the universe. And she described the process she had developed for keeping her precious mystical experiences from being discounted as "just mental illness."

I share her story at length because it contains many aspects that, through one set of glasses, look like "psychosis" and, through a different set, look like "mystical experiences."

WHERE OPPOSITES MEET AND MEAN THE SAME THING
Helene's story, an example of overlapping circles

I would call my experience a swelling of spiritual and psychological energy. I had few resources for conceptualizing and containing it. It was so extreme and so difficult. There was a duality. But it was also brilliantly beautiful.

Among my experiences have been a richly developed subconscious (with many dreams and ghosts), a feeling of being held in the hand of God, writing mystical poetry, feeling the energies of places, giving animate importance to inanimate objects (tarot cards, crystals), glowing, floating (noticed by others), seeing people as angels, and an extreme feeling of openness and love.

We humans are not equipped—or educated—to deal with outpourings of this intensity of spiritual energy. During this kind of swelling of energy, unresolved issues get accentuated. We experience these things as humans, and as humans, we are not suddenly clean or free of issues. Lots of things come along in the process.

I was hospitalized for a "single psychotic episode of unknown origin" after a period of dreaming while awake. During this time I saw the world around me as intensely beautiful. I had several intense, meaningful exchanges with others. I was instructed to spread whole love and adopt a more Zen path for myself.

Eventually I felt that I had to leave the community of my college and undertake a spiritual journey. I was distraught at leaving the people I loved and confused about the nature of the journey.

Because of this, I was hospitalized for ten days in October of 1997, and this hospitalization brought the momentum of my scholastic life to a halt.

All of this has triggered a reassessment of my goals and direction. I am now working toward a functionally spiritual lifestyle. This means a purposeful, primarily self-sufficient, working identity. I know my sensitivity to the divine will play an important role in anything I do.

For me, the hospitalization was a necessary growing point to seeing far—and feeling deeply. The rest of me had to catch up. It has been quite disruptive, but it was necessary.

I define mysticism as the struggle of the finite and human mind-body complex to interpret its realization of the divine, both within and without. It is the drama of a human psyche opening to—and relating to—a wider consciousness, a realization of human brilliancy and beauty, a sensitivity to metaphysical relationships.

I don't feel that anyone really understands what has happened to me. I myself only understand it partially. Perhaps that is why I long to hear the stories of others.

Prior to my breaking point, I had spent time in an area near my college campus in a wonderful, old house. I felt compelled to go on a journey to look for my source. I was talking a lot to my mom about genealogy, trying to put stories together, trying to feel that I was the result of a long progression.

At first, I was well and happy and having positive interactions. Then the names and dates sent me into a downward spiral. It was like I was fixed to the place I was in. I didn't want to leave.

It's strange. I felt I had to crystallize my thoughts. I had to become solid knowledge rather than organic.

At one point, I had an image of the tree in the Garden of Eden, and it was choked by a vine. It seemed to be a battle of the intellect and Spirit. The intellect was choking the Spirit. I made a sauce of amino acids, and it was really salty: it dehydrated me. I was coming away from my humanness and into this information poison. I was conceptualizing information as crystallized and solidified, like a book. It wasn't human. I was confused about my desires.

Two friends brought me to the campus health center. My friends told them that I had stopped buying groceries. It's almost funny. It is so absurd to me that not buying groceries was the point that got attention amidst this vast and intense experience.

But here is where there is overlap with my illness: I thought I had to do this journey in the world—and not in myself. The Source is like a source of a river. It is fearful to look for Source outside of self. I couldn't heal until I acknowledged my emotions. I became whole in myself once I left that community for my journey.

In the hospital, I was given an anti-psychotic medication called xyprexa or olanzapine. I came down while I was on drugs in the hospital. At one point, it felt like I'd had a lobotomy. My decision-making brain was gone, but it is back now.

During the whole experience, I felt a real awareness of light in others in a warm and sensitive way. As a result, my compassion has increased. I feel no judgment of others or of the way others get through life. I now meditate more in silence. I pay more attention to the physical reality of my life. And in the process, my spiritual life also gets more attention.

I used to be more interested in spiritual dogma; now I am more interested in spiritual simplicity. I used to be more interested in complex supernatural forces and how they could be worked with; now I am more content with that which is simple. The supernatural is still important, but I now see it as a different aspect of humanity.

I haven't talked a lot with others about my experience, but I did try to explain it to friends and family. My sister has been helpful. She understands, and I don't have to explain it so much to her.

The responses of others have differed. Some see it as a reaction to stress, saying, "You need to take care of yourself." Others see it as a spiritual experience, saying, "Wow, that's amazing."

Personally, I believe an underlying force culminated in my experience. The power of the experience and my belief in the experience worked together to move me forward.

I have read that our reality is defined by how we grow up, the way we learn to use language, and the ways in which our learning is a shared reality with other people. And yet, although my experience was outside the reality of all that I grew up with, it was absolutely real.

Perhaps my practices during the preceding months had led me to some new beliefs. For example, I had read about being a spiritual animal. And one day I looked in the mirror and saw myself transform into a hawk. It was strange, but I believed it was possible.

How much of our experience is simply symbol that humans have created? And how much is really "out there" and we are simply picking it up? I don't know. But I know that at one point I saw three people as angels. I couldn't touch their wings, but I could see them.

Later, when my mom was upset, I could feel an angel form in my own body. As a kid, I didn't think of angels being around, but now they are real to me. Part of this is metaphor, but perhaps angels represent some of the ways that we have of being helpful to others. Conceptualized in a different way, what I experienced is an increasing of human capacity.

The first night of my hospitalization somebody said, "You're too sane." Everything was just right with me. I had a clear perspective that was *too* clear. Then, the last night, a friend said, "You're *truly* insane."

I believe I was experiencing a duality, a place where opposites mean the same thing. I call it an underworld—not in the sense of a hell but more like seeing both sides of a mirror. Take anger and compassion, for example—it's a whole feeling.

During those days, my sleep was a different kind. For four days, it was a really rich, restoring sleep that lasted for exactly eight hours. Then I would wake up naturally.

One day, my friend was there and I felt very empowered, like music gradually increasing. Everything was beautiful; nothing was ugly. My senses increased. I didn't dislike any food. There was no longer a like or a dislike. Different foods were just different from each other. It's the same with people: we are just different from one another.

Water, too, was very sweet.

It's hard to find words to explain these things. The best words I can find now to describe what happened are *flux, opening, revolution* —everything changed in natural ways. It didn't *feel* sudden, though looking back, it *was* sudden. Not did it feel shocking. I felt in control, but I was *not* in control.

I sensed different identities coming into my presence, such as *Grace* and *As You All* (encompassing all identities). I identified with being an oracle, very mythic. I had the most faith I have ever had. Then from my Widow's Peak (on my forehead), three drops of meaningful water fell.

I had an interaction with someone who said he would bring people to the waterfalls. I was overflowing. I kept spilling some of anything I drank to give some to the ground. It was metaphorical, a image of the Fountain of Truth. It made sense that it would come from what some Eastern religions call the crown cakra, the highest bit of consciousness.

I felt I was in control of myself—and also not in ownership of myself. I would be breathing, and then my breath would close off as if it didn't belong to me. I became very interested in mending and cleaning. I wanted to help people and bring people together. I wanted to see and help situations to work better, but I was not practical about it and didn't know how.

During this time I felt very ambitious. In the integration, I knew my life's work would be healing. But I now realize that I have at least a lifetime to accomplish it. So the pressure is off.

Initially, I rejected any label of illness, but there is an aspect of imbalance and pain that I can't deny. Also, the isolation *is* an ill feeling.

The dreams that I am given are neat. They are a safe place for things to happen. It's a safe distance. I can wake up and choose what to do with them.

I had a friend who was with me through this. In a dream, there was a blinding light all around his body. I was in awe. He said, "Maybe you've just listened to something you have never listened to before," and I hugged him. That connected to a dream from the night before in which I met a blind man and said, "So, it's not bad to lose a sense," and he said, "No." It was good to see the blinding spiritual light around my friend, and good that I could also hug his body.

I have also had several experiences with premonitions and advance dreaming. My mother, my sister, my best friend, and I have relationships conducive to this type of communication. I believe a person sensitive to metaphysical aspects of mundane life might also experience some extrasensory perception. If spiritual revelation is fundamental to the self-process and character of an awakened or stimulated consciousness, then extrasensory perception would be among the acquired tools of the mystic.

Although I do not call myself a mystic, I do aspire to the difficult path of mysticism. I believe developed mysticism requires the support of a teacher or community. Therefore, I am presently striving merely to exercise my ability to be in the world with some simplicity and independence.

So much in such a short time, so many stories and connections!

I talk about these experiences with those I deeply trust, and I have been well received. I treasure these experiences and don't wish to have the skepticism of others color them. Fortunately, more often than not, others' responses actually help to sustain my faith.

I would like to hear more from others about their mystical experiences. I am receptive to hearing about all ways that people grapple with expanding consciousness. We are each blessed and each have our own vocabulary for realizing these blessings. I watch for leadings that promote self-nurturing and self-acceptance. I try to foster strengthening and growth.

I hope eventually there will be a forum for those of us with mystical experiences to share. But in this communication, we will need to be sensitive to the sometimes distracting metaphors or language used to interpret the experience.

Helene considers her "psychotic break" an important part of her opening to higher consciousness. Therein lies a dilemma. Traditionally, mental-health models have seen such experiences as unredeemable suffering, a problem to be fixed. Such experiences have been seen as mental illness, pure and simple. Yet, it seems that such experiences might also be a step toward a positive reintegration at a level of higher consciousness. Certainly for Helene it seems to have resulted in a positive transformation.

At one point, as we talked together, I asked Helene to describe the difference between mysticism and mental illness. She said:

It is like a statue.
When the statue is turned one way,
it is mysticism.
When the statue is turned the other way,
it is mental illness.

I don't know if Helene's perspective is right or wrong, but I decided to suspend disbelief and explore it. I began to probe the raw experience that makes up the center of the overlapping circles shown in figure 2, the experiences that shape the two sides of Helene's statue. What are the overlapping experiences that can, on the one hand, be labeled as mysticism or, on the other hand, be seen as mental illness? *We have raw experiences in our bodies—what determines the names that we give to those experiences?*

In her 1992 essay, "The Relationship Between Schizophrenia and

Mysticism," author Sandra Stahlman observes that the relationship between psychosis and the mystical has been addressed in various ways throughout history. In like manner, in a 1973 essay called "Schizophrenia—the Inward Journey," Joseph Campbell makes a comparison between the journey of the mystic and the journey of the schizophrenic.

In the next chapter, I describe some elements of that journey that have been simultaneously labeled as mystical and pathological. All people do not experience all of these, but they reflect patterns of experience that I heard often as I listened.

Campbell says that schizophrenics have withdrawn from life, have lost touch with things, have no roots, and are cut off from themselves and others. From this detached base, schizophrenics enter into the world of their own fantasies. Schizophrenics, he says, enter the bleak darkness of paranoia while mystics, on the other hand, enter "the dazzling darkness of *metanoia*" (rebirth).

Both feel a need to break away from their social environment. Both set off on a pilgrimage. The pilgrimage may involve a long and dismaying retreat in which there is a chaotic series of encounters that are strange and terrifying. But the schizophrenic and the mystic then go in different directions.

The mystic begins to enjoy encounters of a centering kind, encounters which are fulfilling and harmonizing. This pattern of separation, initiation, and return is common to those who make the journey toward deeper connections.

The mystic and the schizophrenic begin the journey together, but as Campbell suggests, vital differences emerge. And sometimes, if there is to be a life-enhancing outcome, instruction is necessary. "With the aid of a guide," he writes, "we enter what appears to be the menacing and turbulent ocean, and much to our joy and surprise, find that we can swim."

In the chapters ahead, we will look further at the ways in which mysticism and mental illness often constitute not different bodily experiences but rather a series of richly overlapping circles, circles which simultaneously offer the possibility of alienating consequences as well as a deepening spiritual transformation. And as we will see, the outcome often depends on the choices that are made and the support that is offered.

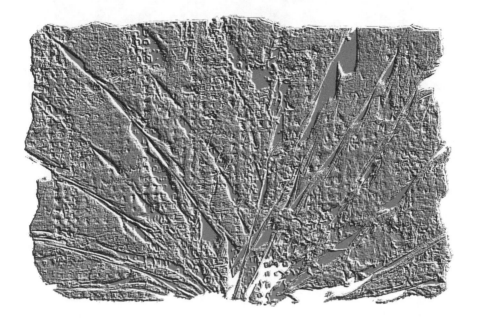

CHAPTER 4

"When, in the course of such a journey, a mystic goes out to the edge—or even leans over the edge—she still finds her way home . . ."

Hearing Voices, Wrestling with Opposites

THOSE WHOSE JOURNEYS are labeled as mystical experiences—and those labeled as mental illness—typically share a number of common characteristics. But I'd like to examine two in particular: Both tend to report a *preoccupation with opposites,* including a persistent effort at reconciling them. And both tend to report *hearing voices.*

We could obviously talk about other commonalities as well, but I want to explore these two specific kinds of experiences in greater detail to give you a better sense of the important issues involved in these overlapping struggles. I hope that as you reflect with me on these two kinds of experiences, you will find greater insight into the enduring question of whether such experiences are empowering encounters with the divine—or simply a destructive and pathological form of mental illness. We may even find that there is a third possible conceptualization, a conceptualization that questions our most fundamental ways of thinking.

Let's look first at the ways in which each of us, in our everyday lives, is constantly RECONCILING OR LIVING WITH OPPOSITES.

In the morning, I half awaken and ask myself: shall I wake up or shall I sleep more? Shall I turn on the light or shall I leave it off? Shall I get out of bed now or shall I stay in bed until later? I go to the bathroom and decide to take a bath now rather than stay as I am. Then I turn on the faucets and decide on hot or cold—more hot, more cold? Thus goes the rest of my day: endless encounters with opposites, endless choices between work and rest, speech and silence, movement or motionlessness. We hardly even notice, for in the everyday physical world, the flow of opposites is usually relatively easy.

Our lives get more complicated, however, when we enter the realm of thought and values. There the apparent opposites that we deal with are more like: attractive/unattractive, male/female, health/illness, true/false. As we enter the spiritual realm, the flow of opposites becomes even starker: right/wrong, chosen/not chosen, hope/fear, fear/love, birth/death, death/rebirth, good/evil. Sorting out opposites such as these can get harder.

As women, especially, we sometimes find ourselves caught in uncomfortable dualities of self: no self vs. self, selfishness vs. selflessness, self-giving vs. self-gaining. But in mystical experience, self and no self are not opposites; rather, they often live together in the same world, in the same space.

In the writings of the great mystics, there is much talk about being selfless. To read such words from a place of duality would threaten one's sense of self and identity. But the selflessness that mystics often speak of is not the same as the selfless, boundary-less world of a psychotic, a place that renders one totally incapable of being a self, for without a boundaried identity, we are unable to function in the world. To bring self and selflessness into one coherent whole is the task.

One participant in my study had undergone twelve hospitalizations before she came to that place where *selflessness* could be defined in ways that she could live with and not be lost in. The selfless language of religion is not helpful to people who have either not yet learned to have a self or whose personal development has not given them a clear identity. We cannot give to God a self, an ego, or a will that we never had. And our attempt to do so can provoke an intense personal crisis.

In the writings of the saints and mystics, I find that many say one thing in one paragraph—and the apparent opposite in the next. Each may describe a different path, but as they move toward spiritual perfection, they seem inevitably to enter a place of wrestling with the fullness of God and their own wholeness. They wrestle with pleasing God—and pleasing their own desires. They wrestle with the spirit and with the flesh.

All of us encounter these struggles on our path to a deeper walk with God. We wrestle with opposites until we come to that place where we are able to see them as parts of a single whole. One of the struggles that hooked me for quite a while was the struggle to understand the power of powerlessness. Is there power in powerlessness? Is there powerlessness in seeking power?

Good and evil are opposites with which all of us eventually have to wrestle. Unfortunately, in that wrestling, many people get lost. I recently heard an astute psychologist say, "The experiences of the mystic and the mentally ill person are often the same in this realm." Yet, while the struggles may be the same, the outcomes are different.

I have heard people describe being pulled as if by gravity to a "place where opposites meet and mean the same thing." They are talking about a place of wrestling, a place of struggle, a place of new understanding, a place of relational insight that opens new levels of truth. The mystic flows through these struggles, finding that place where opposites touch. When, in the course of such a journey, a mystic goes out to the edge—or even leans over the edge—she still finds her way home. She is still moving toward wholeness. Her strength is undiminished.

It is those who get lost—and cannot find their way back—who may be labeled as "crazy." In yielding to the rushing pull of gravity, they may have raced remarkably close to that miraculous place of deepened understanding. But perhaps in their race to truth, they failed to gather the resources they needed to go further on the journey. Quakers call this "outrunning the guide." Or perhaps their flailing struggle caused them to miss the landing place, the meeting place, caused them to lose track of even where they were. Maybe they lacked adequate outer resources. Or maybe they simply bumped up against a societal norm that caused things to come crashing down on them. Whatever the reason, lost in an unfinished journey, they experience the terrors of what is often called mental illness.

In his prose poem, "The Marriage of Heaven and Hell," William Blake seems to explore this same relationship between good and evil:

> Rintrah roars & shakes his fires. . . . Without the Contraries is no progression, Attraction and Repulsion, Reason and Energy, Love and Hate, are necessary to Human existence. From these contraries spring what the religious call Good & Evil. Good is the passive that obeys Reason. Evil is the active springing from

Energy. Good is Heaven. Evil is Hell. . . . As I was walking among the fires of hell, delighted with the enjoyments of Genius, which to Angels look like torment and insanity, I collected some of their Proverbs: . . . Shame is Pride's cloak. Joys impregnate. Sorrows bring forth.

In her psychological interpretation of Blake's poem, June Singer says, "Rintrah is the personification of rage against the status quo, . . . the spirit of prophecy driven out into the wilderness." Singer says that Blake's theory of opposites implies that progression or dynamic development is possible only if the tension between the poles is maintained. She quotes Alan Watts as saying in *The Two Hands of God*:

Polarity is something more than simple duality or opposition. For to say that opposites are polar is to say much more than that they are far apart: It is to say that they are related and joined— that they are terms, ends, or extremities of a single whole. Polar opposites are therefore inseparable opposites like the poles of the earth or of a magnet or the ends of a stick or the faces of a coin.

Singer points out that Jacob Boehme takes a similar position when he writes that "Hell and Heaven are essential to each other, that they exist simultaneously in God. The opposition of the contraries exists in God himself, without which there could be neither light nor darkness."

How do we reconcile good and evil within us? How do we work it out so they get along? In Blake's language, can they marry? And if they can, what are the marriage vows of the heaven and hell within? Might it be that our life force gains its energy from the tension implicit when opposites marry rather than wage war? And are marrying and waging war the only alternatives? Might they not sit down to tea and listen to one another?

In her book, *The Crossing Point*, Mary Caroline Richards describes wrestling with the *daimonic*, those forces that are "not light" in order to release the creativity within us. In classical mythology, the term *daimon* (also spelled *daemon*) refers to that creation place that gives us our creative energy. In classical literature, *daimon* refers to the genius of a person or a place, that which gives rise to its spirit. However, in some dictionaries, it is defined as the demonic, an example of how a word can be used with totally opposite meanings and create confusion.

M.C. Richards describes the struggle thus:

We choose to wrestle with the daimonic because it will increase our self-knowledge, it will help our growth and creativity, and it will enrich our lives and capacity for "good." Our picture of life will change. Wholeness will become a suffering-through of both dark and light. And the meaning of "Judge not!" will become clearer. Truth will include not only the shadow, but the dark "unknowing" out of which consciousness and creativity come. The dark in both senses is the source: dark as the "unacceptable" and dark as intuitive. Our sense of fact expands, our epistemology will develop to include consciously the realms of "spirit knowing": imagination, inspiration, intuition. In tune with this, life is asking us to develop a language true to the facts. This means that we may sacrifice our one-sidedly intellectual language for a language more adequate to the resonances of the double realm. . . . An inner Man stands as an arch between the polarities of being, and transforms them, integrates them. He rides and guides the fire.

None of this is easy, for as she explains elsewhere in her book:

To see in the dark takes new spirit/eyes. It is difficult to work to contain reality, and not to falsify it. We need to be both vulnerable and unwobbling if we are to be open to contacts with the spirit world both dark and light. But when we can do this, each "receiving" and "offering" helps to befriend the realm. To be able to say Yes and No to it. And we ourselves are befriended.

I had a dream in which a tremendous fire was raging clear across the full width of the horizon. . . . It burned steadily. . . . We ran away. . . . One person remained. . . . The fire swept through the landscape, through the house, through the pottery vessels, through the man. I could see the flames coursing through everything, but nothing was being consumed. After the fire had swept through, I returned and the man said, "Everything is still here. Only the color is deepened." And it was so. He was intact, and the pots were richer, deeper and more lustrous in their colors.

These descriptions by Blake, Boehme, Watts, and Richards do not conform to the beliefs I had about reality five years ago, before any changes in my consciousness began to occur. But they do describe very well parts of my own experiences since then, and they seem to reflect rather well the kinds of experiences related by some of the participants in this study.

The **HEARING OF INNER VOICES** is another common characteristic of those whose journey includes either mystical encounters or mental illness. So let's look at that next.

In a 1996 article in *The Journal of Transpersonal Psychology,* psychiatrist Mitchell Liester points out that people have been describing inner voices for thousands of years, across many cultures.

Socrates, for instance, heard voices that advised him against actions not in his best interest, a voice that he called the "daimon" or "the divine." Biblical characters, Christian saints and mystics, the Incas, shamans, and others all over the world have valued inner voices for their guidance, inspiration, and knowledge.

Yet, in contemporary Western culture, inner voices are now largely pathologized. Sometimes I wonder what great losses our culture may have suffered because of our arrogant notion that we have now come to the "right" way of framing this phenomenon.

In his 1996 article on inner voices, Liester, like some other writers before and since, explores alternative ways of working with or understanding inner voices:

> To view such transformations [inner voices] as just the products
> of psychotic symptoms belies an ethnocentric world view. A
> more plausible explanation is that these helpful inner voices
> belong to a separate category of experiences, those which have
> the potential to facilitate growth on individual, interpersonal and
> societal levels.

Inner voices today are often characterized as hallucinations. The term *hallucination* initially applied only to abnormal phenomena, but now it is applied to any unshared sensory experience. The 1994 edition of *The Diagnostic and Statistical Manual,* the standard medical reference manual, defines a hallucination as "a sensory perception that has the compelling sense of reality of a true perception but that occurs without external stimulation of the sensory organ."

Many writers have tried to create other terminology. For example, R.W. Medlicott (1958) used the term *pseudo-hallucination* to describe the hallucinations of the sane.

But despite the efforts of Liester, Medlicott, and others, the hearing of voices is still diagnosed by most practitioners as pathological. In fact, in a classic study on the reliability of diagnoses, research participants went to mental hospitals and claimed only to hear voices. They found that it was unpredictable which label would be used for their diagnosis, but all were diagnosed with a mental disorder of some kind—

and most were hospitalized.

Liester proposes what he calls a hallucination–revelation continuum. His continuum looks something like this:

Pre-personal Experiences	Personal Experiences	Transpersonal Experiences

Hallucinations > Pseudo-hallucinations > Illusions > Perceptions > Imagination > Intuition > Revelations

On the left side of Liester's continuum are experiences that are pathological, regressive, and pre-personal; those on the right side, he describes as healthy, transcendent, and transpersonal.

In his 1993 book *The Spectrum of Consciousness,* Ken Wilber distinguishes pre-personal, personal, and transpersonal states of consciousness. He says that the personal level comes from the rational place that our culture usually defines as "normal." Pre-personal and transpersonal states have in common that they are not primarily rational. He argues that when pre-personal consciousness occurs, it is not rational; the person has not yet attained the personal. The transpersonal state is likewise not rational, he says. Yet it is different from the pre-personal in that the person has reached the personal—and gone beyond it.

Liester views the misidentification of voices as tragic, for it can lead to transcendent inner voices being pathologized. Taken together, Liester and Wilber thus begin to make some valuable distinctions regarding inner voices. These are positive steps in a good direction.

But I note an unresolved problem in their work. Liester recommends further studies of those inner voices that occur "in the absence of pathology." Yet it is difficult to do that kind of study because inner voices *are* pathology in our current system, so "the absence of pathology" itself needs a new definition before any such studies can be carried out.

In a 1989 article called "Inner Voice Experiences: An Exploratory Study of Thirty Cases," M.W. Heery divided such experiences into three types:

- ❖ Inner voices functioning as fragmented parts of the self
- ❖ Inner voices characterized by dialogue, providing guidance for individual growth
- ❖ Inner voices where channels are opened toward and beyond a higher self

She found that some voices do, in fact, have the characteristics described by others as transpersonal experiences. As humans, we go back and forth between states of consciousness. We hear differently, at one time or another, each of the three kinds of voices that Heery notes. We are not in one state or another all the time, and we do not hear just one kind of voice or another. All of this complicates the kind of research that Liester recommends.

Liester says that a defining characteristic of transcendent inner voices is ego transcendence, which is manifested in several ways:

❖ The voices are experienced as originating from an external source and not from one's conscious mind
❖ The voices speak of themselves in the first person, while addressing the individual who hears them in the second person
❖ Dualities are transcended

Wilber says that the ego views the world as an unending series of polarities, but these polarities can be transcended. Inner voices appear self-contradictory from the perspective of the ego, but in fact, they express underlying truths. The rational mind views life in either–or terms, but the transcendent speaks in the language of both–and.

Liester lends further support to this transcendence of dualities in the healthy inner voice when he writes:

> Opposing aspects are seen as inextricably linked aspects of a common unity. Transpersonal experiences thus provide solutions to problems via a glimpse of "the bigger picture." Security and insecurity are viewed not as contradictory, but as inseparable. . . . Fear/desire, aversion/addiction, and countless other dualities are viewed as unavoidable aspects of the human condition. . . . These polarities are transcended.

Liester also suggests similarities between the pathological and transcendent voices. Both are heard with the mind, not the ears. Both appear to have an outside origin, yet both speak the language of the person who hears them. Both may or may not follow disruptions in the normal functioning of the ego (such as from drugs or disease). And both may lead to either beneficial or harmful results.

In light of all this, does a *preoccupation with the reconciliation of opposites* and the *hearing of inner voices* sound to you more like mysticism or mental illness?

It's an absurd question, for the usual image of mental illness and mysticism as two circles with a fine line between them is inadequate. The more I read and the more I listen, the more I am drawn to an understanding of mysticism and mental illness as overlapping circles. Those overlapping circles also make Helene's two-sided statue seem more feasible.

Any effort to put mysticism and mental illness in clear and separate worlds seems a hopeless task, for from the perspective of a person's own initial experiences, the two are often indistinguishable. There are simply too many common elements of bodily experience between that which is genuinely mystical and valuable and that which is genuinely moving an individual in a fragmented and dysfunctional direction.

As I hope I have shown in this chapter, these common experiences are not in themselves either positive or negative. It's what is done with them that matters. It's where they lead the individual that makes the difference.

Personal accounts indicate that the mind can either grow—or blow—from the hearing of inner voices. The same is true with regard to a deep and persistent wrestling with opposites. Which way it goes depends on many factors, including the responses of the individual and the responses of those around the individual. The overriding frameworks and institutions available to a person also make a significant difference. (In this regard, it is important to remember that all frameworks and institutions are human in origin, and each person must seek to find those that best serve his or her needs.)

In the next chapter, I will examine some common stages in the mystical journey. I hope you will join me in reflecting on those critical points at which a person faces a range of choices: choices which can move an individual toward wholeness and integration or, quite tragically, toward terror, alienation, and dysfunction.

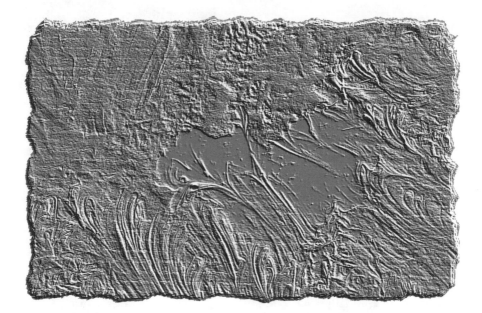

CHAPTER 5

*"Without our protective
'skin,' without our
usual defenses, we
can more readily be
opened to God . . ."*

Radical Moments,
Critical Choices

*W*HITHER SHALL I go from thy
spirit? or whither shall I flee from
thy presence? If I ascend up into
*heaven, thou art there: if I make my bed in hell, behold, thou art there. If
I take the wings of the morning, and dwell in the uttermost parts of the
sea; even there shall thy hand lead me, and thy right hand shall hold me.
If I say, Surely the darkness shall cover me; even the night shall be light
about me. Yea, the darkness hideth not from thee; but the night shineth as
the day: the darkness and the light are both alike to thee.*

Psalm 139:7–12, KING JAMES VERSION

As I suggested in the last chapter, it's difficult to impossible, based
solely on an individual's initial internal experiences, to distinguish a
mystical journey toward God from a journey that is headed in a destructive and dysfunctional direction. They share too many commonalities. Experiences that will lead one individual toward a healthy,
well-contained life may well lead another individual into a miry pit of

mental illness. And often it is not the experiences themselves that make the difference but what we and those around us do with them.

To illustrate the role of some of those radical moments and critical choices, I have tried to compile a generic description of key stages in a journey toward God. This compilation draws from frequently mentioned elements in what I have read, heard, and experienced.

Undoubtedly I have also been influenced by the work of Evelyn Underhill, whose 1960 book, *The Essentials of Mysticism,* described four stages in the mystical journey. She called theses stages purgation, illumination, the dark night, and union. Other authors have described the stages somewhat differently, reflecting the unique individuals they have spoken with and their own linguistic inclinations.

Although the compilation that I offer here uses my own choice of words and my own understanding of what others have shared with me about the key steps in their own journey, you may notice commonalities with the work of both Underhill and others.

Keep in mind that what follows is a generalized description of a journey toward God. It is not the journey of any one person. Because each person's journey is unique, each person's journey may involve only parts of what I describe.

As in any journey involving developmental stages, very few go through the stages in a strictly linear fashion. At any period in our lives, we may be spending more time in one stage than another, but it is not at all unusual for any of us to go back and forth from time to time among the stages.

But as Psalm 139 suggests, whether we are moving forward or backward, whether we are temporarily making our bed in hell or joyfully riding the wings of the morning, God is there. The divine presence is available to us, no matter where we are on the journey.

PRELUDE: FEELING CONNECTED   Many with whom I spoke (though certainly not all) reported that their mystical journeys began in childhood. Often such journeys seem to begin with a simple but deep sense of connection with God. Memorable experiences, even at a young age, often serve to solidify faith.

AWAKENED BY THE LIGHT
Abbie's story, an example of early beginnings

> When I was eight or nine, I had a profound experience. It was very important and real, but I have not shared it until now. I was scared it would be ridiculed.

My dog was ill. I wanted it tended, but it was too late. It had to be put to sleep. As a youngster, I was quite upset that I hadn't been able to stop the dog's death. I went into the woods, cried, and then fell asleep. Later, an enormous light awakened me; it illuminated the woods and comforted me. I did not hear voices as such, but there was a knowing: "You are loved. All will be well."

I had to walk fifteen minutes to get home. As I walked, remembering the light, feeling the knowing, I resolved to help the rejected and neglected people of the world.

It has taken until now, at age 65, for me to share these valuable experiences in my life.

Through elemental experiences such as these, whether in childhood or in later years, we are made ready for the journey. A buffet is spread. Not everyone will partake. Some may only nibble. But God's presence is felt. The curtain is raised. The stage is set.

FIRST ACT: HEARING THE CALL   When we become aware of a change in our lives, when we feel something different happening inside, when we sense that God may be available not just to others but to us, we can become open to that presence. (Of course, some become more opened than others.)

New openings or deepenings (further openings to God) appear to occur most often during times of stress, loss, grief, trauma, or when we are feeling overwhelmed. During these times, our usual defenses are lowered. We are more vulnerable.

It seems that the stronger a person is in terms of those things that are valued in our culture (such as a good job, prestige in the community, or political status), the harder the fall must be to render us vulnerable and thereby open us to change. I am not suggesting a perfect correlation, but there does appear to be a relationship.

Our culture tends to think of vulnerability as a bad thing, something to be avoided. People labeled with psychosis, describing what it is like to be in that place, sometimes talk about it as "skinlessness." They feel exposed. Without our defenses, we become open to more than we can handle.

Outward behaviors when one is feeling vulnerable include shakiness, being quick to tears, not looking others in the eye, and more. We can become vulnerable for many different reasons, but regardless of its cause, the outward behaviors look the same. However, it is important not to assume that one knows what the outward behaviors mean.

As we accept the risk inherent in vulnerability, we discover its gift, for without our protective "skin," without our usual defenses, we can more readily be opened to God. We may sometimes experience openings like this as a result of our own seeking, but more often they come as a gift of grace.

As we are opened, energy flows in: God energy, Spirit energy, Creator energy, creative energy. We develop a sense that we are on a path or a journey. We also gain a sense of living simultaneously, our feet in two realms. While we move through a physical world, we simultaneously flourish in a spiritual world, a world that goes beyond flesh and blood, earth and water. When God's energy flows in, the wall that usually separates the physical and the spiritual comes down. Or it at least has some very major holes poked in it.

This interconnection of the physical and spiritual worlds, this sense that we are following a path that is simultaneously tied to another, is reminiscent of the connection between the conscious and unconscious realms. Just as the conscious realm is only the tip of our iceberg, so too the physical world is only a fragment of the larger world through which we journey. Perhaps there is also a connection here with C.G. Jung's notions of the personal and collective unconscious.

When we are opened to the bigness of the universe, I call it connecting with God. When we are moved beyond the physical world into the mysteries of a larger universe, I call it connecting with the spiritual realm.

It may be through discomforting vulnerabilities, conscious seeking, or unexpected grace. But once we open ourselves to a larger universe, letting God communicate with us in a deeper way, we begin to receive glimpses of the usually hidden realm. For many, such glimpses are great gifts. The ways that God becomes known to us are limitless. Some people report an awareness of the divine presence in the form of help or guidance or consolation in time of need. A person may be sick: God sends healing. A person may be in trouble: God responds.

As these deepenings occur, many other manifestations are often reported. Some people speak of heightened senses. Colors become more brilliant. Internal and external images become more distinct. Internal and external voices become clearer. Sometimes people experience physical manifestations of this energy, such as quaking (which is how Quakers got their name) or *kriyas* (cleansing, embodied movements of yoga).

Bridges between the physical and spiritual realms are often erected. Dreams, for example, tend to become more meaningful. Daydreams, dreams while sleeping, and even lucid dreams which occur while we are awake can connect us to the large mystery of the spiritual realm. The experience of amazing "coincidences" or synchronicity can also provide a bridge, for through such experiences we sense we are part of something bigger than ourselves.

People often have tremendous difficulty describing these experiences. While we often feel a strong desire to tell others, words seem inadequate. Most of us learned learned our vocabulary as youngsters. The words we learned to use were based on our knowledge and our experiences at that time. They were symbols for objects and experiences that we thought we understood. But as we are opened to a larger range of experiences, and as we encounter deeper mysteries, sometimes the meanings of the words we learned as youngsters no longer seem adequate. We are no longer sure what these words might mean for others. Old assumptions are thrown into question. Perhaps that is why lyrical writing, poetry, drawing, and painting sometimes become the preferred means of expression.

Frequently, the intellectual processes on which we once relied now seem grossly inadequate for framing or communicating our experiences. For example, logic and linearity in thinking, which may have served us well in the past, no longer appeal. Likewise, our concentration may change. Those things that once consumed us may be set aside. Our focus may be different. Those who experience a mystical calling often move from concentrating on matters of status, prestige, or money toward concentrating instead on love for others, the importance of compassion, the need to work against injustice, or the need to get food to hungry people. There is often a sense of needing to do God's work, the work that God intends us to do.

Some (though not all) who hear the call report experiences that are commonly thought of as psychic, such as out-of-body experiences, extra-sensory perceptions, or pre-cognition. These may involve a sense of the presence of God, but they usually occur in relation to other people. They seem to be possible because we have been opened to that which we usually do not have access to, which is the spiritual realm.

As we go deeper, the energies become more powerful, the voices and visions continue and have a stronger influence. In many ways, time and space boundaries are altered—or transcended. These experiences are often numinous and ineffable, sacred and not explainable with words. Many Christians experience the Light or Jesus or angels in clearer form. However, espousing Christianity (nor any other religious tradition) does not appear to be a prerequisite, nor does conscious seeking. Some have been graced with God's presence even while claiming atheism as their religion.

At some point, as we begin to hear the call, a "dark night" experience may occur. Ultimately, such an experience is much treasured. But at first, it can seem quite frightening. It doesn't happen for everyone, but for those for whom it does occur, it is like having your life stripped, much as the layers of an onion are stripped away. And with this stripping comes dramatic changes. For some, there may be a change in vocation. For others, every aspect of their lives may be turned around. And these changes typically occur with what is almost a drastic sense of necessity. It's not coercion. There is choice involved. But the choice grows out of a deep sense of knowing the consequences of not making the needed change.

These dramatic changes can often lead to a profound sense of loss. The normal human response to loss is grief, often accompanied by denial, rage, depression—and eventual acceptance. It's only natural that in our spiritual journeys, we remain human. As humans, we remain vulnerable to all the usual human conditions.

In retrospect, this "dark night" is often seen as one of the most treasured and valuable points on one's spiritual journey. But when one is in the midst of it, especially if one is fighting against it, it can be most painful and difficult. Rage and terror may abound.

A hard part of this dark night is the apparent pull toward nothingness. At some point, we must let go of the pain of the trauma we have encountered. For some of us, our embodied, physical lives have essentially been demolished. All is gone except the pain. This leaves us in an excruciatingly vulnerable place. On one level, it seems as if the only thing that we have to hold on to is our pain. So when we hear a call to empty our souls, our deepest fear is triggered: the fear of nonbeing. It may feel like we are being called to nothingness, and nothing could be more frightening. Perhaps that is why the writing and thinking of those who encounter such a call is often filled with the language of *the void* and *the abyss.*

Here is where faith is most needed: our own faith as well as the faith of others. At times, because we are human, our own faith will falter. That's why it's so important to have friends around us who can have faith *for* us when our own faith is shaken. If we have that kind of friendship, it is a gift. Many lack it.

Even with faith, hearing the call is never easy. Are we really to give the pain to God—and live in trust—even when God seems to have abandoned us? Are we really to jump into the nothingness—with nothing but faith—when there is no outward evidence that it makes good sense to do so? Are we really to trust God, even when we can't feel any divine presence? It defies all logic, all rationality, and all the rules that are usually good rules to live by. But the answer on all counts is yes. It is the hardest part of the journey for many, but we are to give God the pain, enter the apparent nothingness, and fully trust that God is there.

At this point, we have to *know* God's presence, even if we can't feel it. If we are not to shut our ears to the call, we have to have come to that place where we *know* that the darkness that we feel is warm and good and full of creation energy, even when we can't see it, even when our minds can't understand it.

Several times the Gospels describe Jesus as saying, "Let those who have ears, hear." We'll never get to the end of the first act of the spiritual journey if we aren't willing to hear the call of the divine presence. And we must hear it so well, hear it so thoroughly, that no matter where we find ourselves, no matter what pain and anguish we feel, we will *know* that God is there. In this respect, I cannot overemphasize the importance of Psalm 139, which functions as a reminder that God is present in our lives—no matter what, no matter where, no matter why.

When we reach that faith, when we accept that reality, we fly.

SECOND ACT: ENTERING THE CLEARING   How we frame and understand the pain and the call to nothingness that we encounter at this point is critical. The choices are to see the pain as having a redeemable purpose in our lives—or as having no purpose, just unredeemable pain to be stopped in any way possible.

Is it possible that purpose/no purpose exists on a continuum, with many points between end points? I think so. Our pain may have some of each: purpose and nonpurpose. Can we be clear which is which? Not always. But often the pain reflects a radical moment, a choice point in our path. For many people, the choices that lie before them have, until this point, not even been conscious. Yet, through some remarkable means, we are now led from the tangle of limbs and trees. We leave the maze of rising brush and dangling vines and enter a new clearing, a clearing that we had not seen before, a place that calls for a new decision, a new direction. For some, it may be a decision to live or to die. For others, it may involve how to earn money, how to bring more love into the world, or how to heal a broken relationship.

Such decisions must be pondered from a deep place. At this fork-in-the-road place, in the midst of this sacred clearing, ordinary decisions won't do. We are drawn to a clearer sense of self as God created us. Some call this the True Self, but that suggests that there is also a False Self, and to me, that seems drastic and condemning. So I prefer to speak of being in touch with a deeper self, the part of me that is closest to that creation energy in my soul. All of me has served at some point in my life to do some of the work that I needed to do on this earth. But when I reach this sacred clearing, some of my habits, some of my trauma, some of the programs given to me as a child to get me to conform must go. They go not because they are evil or bad or false. Actually, they need to be celebrated and thanked, for they all served well to get me where I am. It's just that now it is time for me to get in touch with what Quakers call "that of God in me." To Jungians, it might be the "Self." To others, it might be "the Real Me." But it is more than "me" in the ordinary sense. It is the "me" that has been most fully shaped and called by the Light, by the Spirit, by the divine Creator.

Upon entering the clearing, some choose to do this work—and some do not. For many lives, this is the turning moment, the point at which we choose which path to follow. Having heard the call, we can reorder our steps in harmony with the divine—or not. Having heard the call, we can reach deep into that new world that has been opened to us and move forward in wholeness and faith—or not.

Having entered this clearing, this remarkable new opening in the forest, some become stuck in a state of alienation, isolation, and disconnection. Instead of drawing on the divine to move forward, they stand still. It's as if a "bell jar slams down." They feel trapped. They feel as if there is no way to reach either God or other humans. Nor do they know how to get out of that state. Others, catching glimpses of that alienation and isolation, begin a new movement toward God, toward a life of gratitude for everything that happens and everything that is, finding a sense of purpose for all of it, knowing in an almost intimate way that God is present no matter what.

I am tempted to call the first response *mental illness* and the second, *mysticism*. However, I cannot safely use that terminology, for in my profession, mental illnesses are typically diagnosed long before this point. Many people are diagnosed with psychosis based solely on the kinds of experiences I described as being a normal part of the first act. Visions, voices, presences, and energies are likely to be labeled as mental illness early on, without any consideration of their potential for a positive or negative effect on one's life.

So I will use different language for the two responses. I will call the first the path of alienation and the second the path of connection. It is here, in the midst of the clearing, that we make our choice. It is here, in the midst of the clearing, that we set our direction. Up to this point of decision, people who have had experiences identified as mystical and people who have been characterized as having a mental illness can relate equally well to the journey as I have described it.

Along the way, the ability to function in the world and not make other people feel too uncomfortable seems to be critical in keeping oneself from being formally labeled with mental illness or informally described as "crazy." Some people have the strength to contain their experiences of God, and they enjoy positive support from the people around them. For others, the experience is too intense or too foreign or too frightening. They cannot contain it. And those around them express discomfort with what is happening. All of this can influence not only the label that is applied but even the actual path that is available.

ACT THREE: FOLLOWING THE PATH   Those who follow the path of alienation often begin by feeling called or drawn to something different. Doors are opened. For a time, they may struggle with a "dark night." And before long, they are led into that remarkable clearing, that radical moment when one can move toward greater wholeness and connection. But then something interferes with their answering or with their going toward the life-giving call.

The most common problem that I hear is that when a person felt the energies, heard voices, saw visions, felt presences, or needed to engage in some art form, others began defining the person as "crazy."

The message that these things are "crazy" can take many forms. It may be a child, needing great amounts of your time. It may be a spouse saying you don't need to waste money on paints because that is frivolous and finances are tight. It may be a member of the clergy insisting that God "spoke" to people in Bible days but that is not how God works any longer. It may be a therapist saying these are hallucinations and you need medication to stop them. The message not to honor our inner guide, not to honor the call that would move us toward God—toward our own unique purpose, toward our own True Self—can come in many different ways.

But when we do not honor the divine call, we often become impotent in our worldly actions. When we are pressured to pay more attention to how we are "being" in the world, our "doings" may suffer. When we are hindered from pursuing the new possibilities that have been opened to us, our ordinary accomplishments in the "normal," physical world often require extreme amounts of effort.

It doesn't take much more resistance until our lives go from impotent to alienated. We come to a place where we cannot connect with God or with even other people. God's presence is not felt or known. Outward behaviors that get one labeled psychotic, or even criminal or drug-addicted, become understandable when, inwardly, one is living in this place of alienation.

Others enter that remarkable clearing and choose the path of connection rather than alienation. They have experienced too much to turn back. They have tasted too freely of a deeper world, a greater reality. Because they have learned to be open and receptive, they hear and answer the call.

This place of responding to our call is different from what is taught in many religions as "obedience" to God. It is not a matter of submitting to an all-powerful father figure who will punish us if we are bad. It is rather a process of letting go of those parts of ourselves that served us well in the past but are not functional now. It is a process of finding that strongest part of ourselves, that part that is God within us, our truest identity, our fullest potential. It is that which speaks to us when we sit in silence and know it is good.

The language around "obedience," "giving up ego," and "being selfless" is very confusing. Such confusions have caused harm to many people. Living in the presence of God requires a strong sense of our uniqueness, a strong sense of our truest identity, a confidence in the power of that creation ability that we have when we are connected with God. One must go through the developmental stages of becoming a strong ego and having a strong will before one can give it to God. It is a mistake to teach obedience to God as a strong patriarch who requires total submission, especially before a person has a chance to become a strong and well-developed person. At least, I must say that these teachings caused *me* much difficulty along the way. Not only have I concluded that they do not work for me, but I have heard many others say the same.

There is a temptation to interpret what I have described as justification for the kind of pride that makes me feel better than another. That is not the intended interpretation. On the journey, we all become broken and must humbly ask for the healing and strength we need.

Much ego strength is needed to contain the energy of the Spirit. If one has not developed a strong sense of one's own unique identity, it is unlikely one can contain that energy, and one's behaviors are likely to lead to trouble.

Ego strength gives one a sense of who to talk to about what—and when. It gives one a sense of caring for the self and the body that God made us to be, the temple of God's Spirit. When one has sufficient ego strength, there is a built-in meter that seems to guide behavior away from those things that might be destructive to God's temple. One friend called it the "appropriateness meter."

At the fork in the road, at the clearing in the forest, the input of others can also make a difference. Friends, spiritual directors, or therapists can help a person to learn to listen and trust their own inner guide. They can celebrate the journey. They can find the gifts when the person, in their pain, cannot. They can have faith with the person when that person has lost faith. They can provide the supportive container when the person's own ego strength is faltering.

Grace from God, combined with our own ego strength and the generous support of others, can allow us to move from the clearing in the forest onto a new path of connection. Life becomes not just good but very good. Faith is increased. Purpose becomes more clear. The obstacles in our path are moved, and life goes forward more jubilantly and more abundantly. We are freed to move back into the world of service, and our service is both more efficient and more effective.

We must remember, though, that none of this happens on a totally linear path. Our return to the world may be only temporary; there is much back and forth movement along the way. As we keep traveling this journey, the path takes us to a deepening desire both for God and for living in God's will. Some describe this as a process of abdicating one's own will for the sake of obedience to God's will. But for many of us, the journey leads to the depths where God's will and our own will become one. When we move with God along our own unique path, we feel a deep sense of co-creation.

For most who make the journey, there is a "knowing" of what one needs to do, and sometimes this "knowing" is that one is in the midst of a waiting time. For people who are "doers" by nature, such waiting is very difficult. For people who have developed their identity around giving to others, this period of "required self-centeredness" can seem nearly impossible. But until the time is right to go back into the world of service in a more God-centered and healthy way, premature efforts to return to service will be ineffective. Many who return to service after a period of "waiting" report that everything in their lives up to that point seems to have been put there to prepare them for this service. A prepared mind, an open heart, and space in one's soul for God-energy seem to be required. Consolations, including a sense of God's presence, are the gifts that sustain the journey.

In moving along the path of connection, some people have not only experiences of the Light but also experiences of what some call "darkness." For those who pursue the path of connection, the word *darkness* is anything but pejorative. Some use it to describe a place of transformation and renewal, "the dazzling darkness of metanoia." Others see it as a comforting place, a warm and cozy place of closeness to God. For still others, the darkness is a quiet place where they can experience moments of escape from the intense scrutiny of the Light.

For those on the path of alienation, darkness is more often associated with terror, rage, or depression, and these conditions can range from mild to very severe in intensity. For some on the path of alienation, darkness is associated with separation from God or with what is often called sin. A few say that in darkness they have had glimpses or "brushes with evil."

Because of these different understandings, to say that one has experienced "darkness" has little communication value in and of itself. Those who walk different paths may use the term with radically different understandings.

In addition to its references to "darkness," some mystical writing contains erotic language as well. In my interviews with others about their experiences, one woman told me of having sex with God. She believed that to have come from "sexual demons," and she saw it as part of her mental illness. Another said that her most precious mystical experience was the sense of having sex with Jesus.

We may initially be inclined to freak out at such talk—or at least find these descriptions very fascinating. But as I explored the eroticism in the mystical journey, I came to understand it better.

On the mystical journey, many of the voices, visions, healings, and presences come with bursts of energy. The energy is of the Spirit, the energy of our Creator. It is creative energy given to us for continued creation. As we come to live in the place within us that is our truest self, the place that Quakers call "that of God within us," we gain a greater and greater sense of co-creation with God. Much energy is given to us for that task. And as we co-create with God, the communion with God is intense. Eventually, as two wills are joined into one, union occurs. In its purest form, sexuality is about union and creation; it is the drive toward creation. So it is not surprising that those who are led along such paths sometimes rely on erotic imagery to describe the exhilaration of their journey with the divine.

But that sense of connection, that sense of union, is seldom an end in itself. For many people, the experience of union with God is the beginning of a journey back into the world to do that work which is now both God's and their own.

For those who follow the path of connection, for those whose mystical journey is healthy and strong, work is no longer something one does to build one's career, gain prestige or status. Work is no longer for pleasing others or for conforming to rules. One's real work becomes the living out of that sense of co-creation with God.

The journey is to *be* with God, doing what our unique calling calls us to do. The doing will be different for each of us, for the connection that each of us makes with the holy reflects the unique spirit that God has put in us all. What an important part of our lives this journey is!

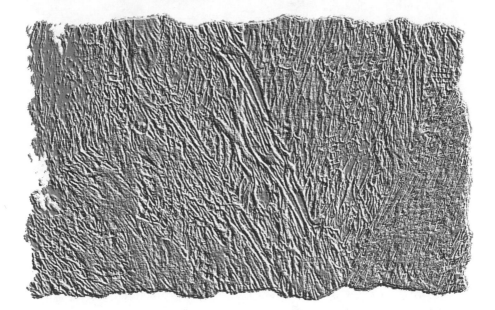

CHAPTER 6

*"That which is
mystical doesn't
contort what we know
as reality: it only
adds a
dimension . . ."*

Wrestling with God
in the Unknown

RADICAL MOMENTS AND critical
choices mark the journeys of those
whose lives weave through the
sometimes confusing maze of experiences that some see as mysticism
and others see as mental illness. As I said in the last chapter, the journey is seldom linear. At times, we may go forward, backward, and side-
ways—and even around in circles.

But typically there is an extended time of HEARING THE CALL, a time
in which one's experiences can be both terrifying and liberating, a time
in which something beyond one's self seems to be tugging and calling
in ways that may not always be well understood, a time in which one's
experiences seem to go beyond the realm of the ordinary.

Eventually, after the exhilaration and uncertainty of the first act,
there comes a time of ENTERING THE CLEARING. Here is the point at which
one emerges from the tangle of the forest into an open place, a place
of emerging awareness, a place of conscious decision. Some enter the
clearing with deep inner strength. Others come with looming uncer-

tainties. Some come surrounded with the love and support of a caring community. Others feel nothing but rejection and abandonment.

From that radical clearing, from that critical juncture, a new direction is set. And so act three typically becomes a time of FOLLOWING THE PATH. That path can be the path of spiritual integration and wholeness. Or it can be the terrifying and oftentimes destructive path of alienation and despair. Actually, it is not unusual for a person to go back and forth between these paths for a long while.

Some of us hear God calling, enter the clearing, and know almost immediately what path we are to follow. It is sure and sweet and clear. For others, however, much preparation awaits. We may long to move forward in our journey. We may ask, beg, even plead for clarity. But God's timing is not ours. Sometimes God's timing is to wait. Sometimes, for whatever reason, we have to slow down. Sometimes, for whatever reason, we are not yet ready.

Preparation for the unknown is often far from our basic nature. Many of us find it hard to abide in God's presence. It's frustrating when God's pursuit of us does not immediately lead to where we are to be. We don't easily take to scratching our head in the clearing, wondering if we really heard a call, wondering what path we are to take, wondering when the time will come to move forward in our journey.

Many of us have been served well by a deep inner drive. Our culture fosters a goal-oriented attitude toward life. I know that for me, it served well. In the physical world, it helped me rise. It helped me reach and achieve beyond anything that would have been predicted by my earliest years.

Yet participants in my project spoke repeatedly of the necessity of wrestling with God—sometimes for an extended period of time, sometimes far longer than they initially felt comfortable with.

Dear God, I hear your call.
I know not where you call me.

Where are you, God?
And where am I to be?
Show me!

Wait, you say.
I am not patient: it is not my nature.
Wait, you say.
I wait.
And my nature wrestles.

Through this extended wrestling, many feel a change in their lives. By waiting, by abiding, by not rushing forward, we are exposed to a larger piece of reality. And more often than not, this larger reality does not fit with our previous style of achievement in mainstream, contemporary culture. But after being opened to something bigger, there is no going back. Neither is there any going forward as the old person that we once were, for when we finally hear God's call and when we finally are ready to emerge from that clearing in the forest, it is the demands of the world that we leave behind.

It is almost as if a birthing happens. Emerging into new life requires wrestling. The wrestling may be a breaking through the shell that surrounds us, as a baby chick must do. It may be wrestling through the birth canal, as a newborn baby must do. The labor can be relatively easy, or it can be arduous. But from such a birthing— whether short or long, moderate labor or heavy—creation comes.

Such a birthing involves pain, but the pain serves us in knowing the joy of co-creation with God. You will hear words about this kind of wrestling toward a new birthing in the two stories that I share in this chapter.

After a time of wrestling with the unknown, and a relatively mild labor, Marjie was called into a traveling ministry. She has had much support through the process, and she continues to have many around her to help with clearness.

Susanna, on the other hand, had a longer and more arduous time of labor. She has had to deal with much fear and intensity of experience, but she has learned to garner the resources she has needed. As a result, her ministry is now coming forth.

To clear the way for doing God's work, both have had to deal with the aftermath of early life trauma. Both have had mystical experiences. And both have had to wrestle in the unknown, not knowing where they were being led. Here are their accounts.

DISCERNING THE WORKINGS OF THE LIGHT
Marjie's story, an example of a relatively moderate time of wrestling

Because of the strength of my own experiences and the changes in my life that have resulted from those experiences, I have learned to be very conscious of the need for anchors and the role of spiritual discipline and discernment. The mystical has brought me back to the Bible and to learning how much Christ has to teach us about the workings of the Inward Light, about the nature of taking up the cross, even about the nature of "demons."

I have found that words of early Friends make wonderful spiritual guides, as do the writings of various Buddhist monks.

Mysticism is the word I use to speak about the times when God touches human lives, those times when individuals experience something, however gentle, of Divine Love. Not all extrasensory experiences are mystical, and the mystical is not always a dramatic encounter with visions or voices. But moments exist when there is no question of God's presence.

God's message can lead to a clear message for the individual, and one's life may be changed forever by such an experience. But more often, the Spirit moves gently, in light nudges and movements, which are easily ignored. Discernment—whether of the still, small voice or of visions—helps show us the source and the meaning of such events. The true voice of God leads us in ways consistent with truth, love, the fruits of the Spirit, and the way of the cross. It offers us a deep, inward peace, even when we are asked to undertake extremely difficult tasks. That's why, for me, the discernment process is so important. At times, it may involve discussion with friends, a Friends Meeting, or a special clearness committee. When a leading arises that involves others, it's also appropriate for consideration at a business meeting.

The first time I was aware of the mystical was over six years ago. I was in a meeting for worship after my father died. As I sat in worship, I felt embraced by love, an almost physical feeling of God's arms around me. This let loose tears—and simultaneously filled me with joy. The worship was filled with messages, and each one spoke directly to me. The meeting was one I had never attended before, and all those who spoke were total strangers. Yet out of that worship grew a clear call to ministry, which I am still living out and learning about. Out of that worship also came an understanding that I needed to take direct steps to change the way I relate to those around me.

That night I was up most of the night writing. I wrote a letter to mend a damaged relationship. I wrote another which laid out my sense of a call to ministry. This letter also included the clear sense that I was to ask for a committee of clearness and support and that I was to seek professional counseling. The latter was not because I felt "crazy" but because I needed to address some painful abuses of the past. When I returned to Portland after my father's memorial service, I asked three people to be part of this committee. All three immediately agreed. They met with me monthly for a year and a half while I tried to work out what this call meant in my life and tried to learn to speak what I could of God.

I have also had a few experiences that I have only reluctantly come to call visions, and there was one time when I heard a voice. These, for me, have been deeply moving tastes of the divine. They shake me. I was not able to speak of them for weeks, months, or perhaps years.

Such experiences are rare and unexpected gifts. They tell me much of my relationship with God, with Christ. They are on occasion the root of a message that is shared in meeting for worship. It is as if images, rather than words, seem to rise within me when I am deeply centered in worship and when something more than words is present to me. I am an author, and these images have resulted in some of the most richly creative aspects of my own writing.

I have a friend who is an illustrator. I spoke with her about this, and for her, it is different: she finds that words are the usual starting place for her art. She sits with the words of a book in prayer—and the painting emerges. I find the opposite. The images come first. Then words speak to and from the images.

These images do not evoke "wow, this is neat" or other expressions that I associate with drug-related visions. Dreams are perhaps the closest experience to visions, but visions are different. They have a different taste. I am clearly awake and aware of where I am and what is happening around me. They last no time, yet they have an intensity and an endlessness to them. They feel very much as if they are coming from other than myself, whereas dreams normally feel like part of me.

I have been blessed with dear friends who have been willing to listen and support me even when they did not understand. Speaking about anything related to my faith has been intensely difficult for me. Friends have had to listen to me stammer, and they have had to learn to hold their tongues while I took a seemingly infinite amount of time to speak—and still could not say what I wanted to say. Their struggle to understand what was happening was probably related to my own clear difficulty in speaking of all this, as well as the fact there had been a distinct, though certainly not aberrant, change in my behavior.

The change in my relationships with those closest to me was abundantly clear, and those new relationships were so full of love that it was hard for me—and fortunately for others as well—to doubt the reality of my call.

Initially, I seemed able to express myself much more clearly in writing than in speaking. I knew I needed to work at oral communication as well. All through this multi-stage process, friends were patient, supportive, reassuring. They asked questions gently and suggested ways I might consider what was going on. Mainly they listened and offered of themselves when it was appropriate. Their willingness to be vulnerable—and to learn from my experience—was invaluable.

I have now been released by my Friends Monthly Meeting for my work, and I have a support committee of Friends which meets with me regularly. None of these Friends have ever had mystical experiences, and none had been on this kind of committee before, so we have all been learning. It was important to me that they were getting something positive from being on this committee and were not just participating to "help" me. It was also constructive for me that they each had quite different understandings of their faith and thus did not push me in any one direction but rather allowed me to find my own authentic expression.

Some of the most valuable lessons I have learned have been from the writings of early Friends. I have learned much about the inward struggles that many experienced once they encountered the Light of Christ. The Light shows us the darkness within and the Light shows us how we might find healing and life. Their wrestlings taught me much and gave me hope. I have also learned much from formal spiritual direction, in addition to professional counseling. Both have been part of my growth and have been helpful in easing the changes in my life.

Since that time, I have been fortunate to find myself surrounded by a wonderful community, which includes several profound mystics. We learn from each other and support one another—and occasionally hurt one another—but continue to be willing to be vulnerable, sharing from the deepest part of ourselves and being as transparent as possible to the love of God.

Despite all this, I rarely call *myself* a mystic. To label oneself in that way seems pretentious—and not mine to claim. I have also become clear that, as tempting as it may be, seeking after the more numinous mystical experiences is not what I am about or what we are about as Friends. Rather we are called to live out lives that are in tune with the Spirit and faithful to the will of God.

I had first thought that the call to ministry was a call simply to speak in worship when moved. Before that time, I had always refused to speak in meeting. But it turned out to be much broader, and it expanded to include much speaking and traveling in the ministry, as well as the extensive writing that I am now doing.

The initial experience also led me to read extensively about

Friends, especially about Friends who had had similar experiences, in order to understand what was happening to me. Since then I have written two books, including one on Quakerism, as well as a pamphlet and multiple articles. And I am now in the midst of another book. I left my work as a transportation consultant and am writing and traveling among Friends full time. On occasion, my visions become integrated directly into my writing or speaking, for they tell me much about my relationship with God and about my faith.

I have never been labeled with a mental illness, nor has anyone close to me. I hear of others who have had such an experience, but I am not close enough to know how to respond or to relate to such events. The one experience I have had with someone who had experienced both the "mystical" and a confinement to a mental hospital was when I was traveling in the ministry. One evening I was speaking about mysticism at a meeting after a potluck. A man sitting across from me started to interrupt me with great intensity to relay his experiences. As he did so, he also spoke about how he had been in and out of mental hospitals. The tension in the room was thick as he spoke. It turned out this man had recently started to participate in various meeting events and had been quite disruptive.

I responded to him out of a very centered feeling. I certainly did not have any experience in such things—and I am not sure at all what I said. But as we spoke, others joined in and we talked some in the whole group about mental illness and the mystical. One woman, in particular, was helpful as she shared her experience living in Africa and how some tribes dealt with mental illness in a gentle way that would result in only limited harm to the individual or the village. That evening there was not the deep sharing which often came as I spoke about mysticism, but it seemed like a rich evening in a very different way, and the hostility and tension seemed to melt as the evening went on.

Many times I have heard others describe their religious mystical experiences. Perhaps the fact that I am speaking from my own experience allows others to risk talking about their lives as well. Sometimes this happens in large groups. Other times it is in small groups. Occasionally I have led groups purposefully asking such questions. I also have heard many experiences in private conversations. My own vulnerability in this, combined with a willingness to listen, seem to be central to allowing opportunities for others to speak.

In practice, I seem to use a number of internal "tests" to

determine whether such sharing is OK. One of these tests involves the setting and the purpose for our being together. I am most comfortable in small groups or one-on-one, where there is an understanding both of confidentiality and that I am not in any kind of therapy role. I listen for the tone of voice and the feeling—whether it is confusion, intense desperation, or whatever. I tend to ask myself, is there a calm center? What is the flavor of the experience and the individual's response?

Most of the people I hear simply need someone to speak to. They want confirmation of simple, gentle experiences or times when they have known a sense of the oneness of all life. Most often, I am in the position of encouraging people to recognize the presence of God in their lives in gentle ways. Other times, I am with those who have had deep, intense, or difficult experiences, but often these have been people with considerable knowledge, strength, and resources in this area.

The mystical, as I understand it, is central to who we are as Friends. Coming to recognize leadings, and the voice of God both amidst the ongoing chaos of daily life and in our business meetings, is central to who we are as a Society of Friends. I am most interested to learn about how Friends today understand this—and how we might teach one another more about being faithful to the Spirit.

I am also interested in the question of "Quaker mysticism" and how it relates to "Christian mysticism" among liberal Friends. Our spiritual ancestors had no question that it was the Light of Christ working in our lives and that the workings of this Light could readily be distinguished from other—perhaps evil—spirits, perhaps even what we might call mental illness. Making this all alive and relevant for Friends today is very much a central question for me.

Marjie's birthing was relatively easy. It may be that one's wrestling with the unknown is never fully over, but the labor that brought Marjie to the new path onto which she had been called went relatively smoothly. In this she was blessed: she had many who were willing to listen and to help her discern her calling into a ministry of traveling among Friends.

With the help of her friends, her meeting, her support committee, and others, she struggled with discernment of the Spirit(s). She talks freely about how helpful she has found the writings of early Friends, especially as they describe their own wrestling with the issues related to a call to ministry. She highlights the importance of this process and the important ways in which she has come to her own unique findings.

Marjie has learned the settings and contexts in which she is comfortable listening to the experiences of others, and she recognizes and acknowledges those situations that lead to her own discomfort. Through her own wresting with the unknown, she has also found what she needs to be separate from—and what she would label as illness or even as evil.

LIVING INTO THE MYSTERY
Susanna's story, a journey toward consolation

I do not label myself as a mystic. But I suppose the experiences that I want to share *are* mystical. It's the label that bothers me.

My first experience occurred when I was fifteen. I was sleeping at a friend's house. We were in a church youth group together. In the middle of the night, she started telling me that God had failed her and she was giving up on God. I was spoken through as I answered her. It was like an alien inhabited my body, and it lasted for about two minutes. The voice said things that I didn't even know about. She was chastised, and then the presence left, and I was left to deal with this situation. It was very weird, and needless to say, I quickly put it in the let's-forget-about-that bin.

More typical are the vision experiences that I have had. I work in images in my Quaker meeting and in psychotherapy, so images and metaphors are not unusual for me. But I consider the experiences that I am about to describe as mystical because the depth of meaning was so profound and because they have had the effect of changing me and my life in quantum ways.

Once, while in meeting for worship, during a time when I was doing incest-recovery work, I had an image of myself in a padded cell. I was catatonic, rocking in a corner. Suddenly, the cell went up to the fourteenth floor and sprouted a window. It was not me directing these images. I saw a tapestry, radiantly beautiful. It was small and full of color. It came over gently and wrapped itself around me. I knew I was loved, safe, healed. I also felt forgiveness for my abuser. That was a particular surprise because I had been so angry. The image was spiritually transforming and healing, especially the surprise feeling of forgiveness. It was a turning point in my relationship with my abuser.

Another remarkable incident occurred shortly after the Gulf War broke out. I heard an announcement about a gathering of Friends on the East Coast, and I *knew* that I had to go. I had a new job at the time—with no time off and many obstacles. I went to my new boss and told her that I felt I had to go. Amazingly, she said OK.

In hindsight, I can see why I had to go. At this gathering, I gave a vocal ministry about a vision. I saw a fjord, a glassy lake—beautiful, incredible beauty. In the middle of the lake, a boulder was hurled down. People in meeting were outraged by the defiling of the lake, but we could not move the boulder. I saw that the boulder rested on each offense we all do to each other. In the vision, I waded in and got two pebbles and walked to shore. Others joined in and eventually the stone fell down and was absorbed by the water—forgiven. It felt like a prophecy about the war. War, like the boulder, is bigger than we can handle, but we must each do what we can.

Another time, in meeting for worship during a workshop that I was attending, I had the experience of not just seeing light, like sunlight, but I and the light were the same. I was it. All time and space and sense of self disappeared. When a bell rang to end the experience, I burst into tears because I didn't want to leave it.

Three Brethren women were with me at this same workshop, and they knew something had happened. They sat quietly with me and gently asked me to say what had happened. Their questions were just to get the story out. They weren't trying to evaluate it. That was great! To have their love, curiosity, concern, and recognition that something had happened was very helpful.

I have also had an experience of being taken up into God. This happened when I was grieving, and the prevailing image was darkness. There was a texture like a horse's muzzle when feeding. The enveloping darkness comforted me simply by its truth, the truth of my grieving.

In another vision, I was stuck in a room with no doors or windows. I was seeking a crack or some way out. I cried out for help and God gave me a stone bench. I was ungrateful. There was a sense of dialog between me and God, although God was not answering my questions. I tried to find what to do with the bench. Then, in misery, I sat on the bench and cried. When I opened my eyes, I saw fog, like that dry ice thing in bad theater, It was beautiful, swirling, captivating. The more I watched, the more it took the shape of a giant lion's head. I complained, and the lion listened with empathy, compassion, and love. I poured myself out. Then, there was nothing else to pour. I felt tired and sad, but not trapped anymore. The fog left, the lion left. I walked off into the gray area of a park. I had the sense of having grieved over something and that now I could get on with life. I have told this story to others, and it seems to touch them in important ways.

Psychic experiences are different. They don't involve God. For example, when I was in my early twenties, I was traveling through Europe on the train. In Morocco someone put gas in the cabin of the train, drugged us, and robbed us—this actually happened! I woke up after the drugging with a sense of profound violation. I had to call my mother, even though it was 4 a.m. But even before I had called her, she *knew* something had happened.

I have had other ESP experiences like that.

One time a partner was trying to communicate through ESP. She sent me a message to call her. I sent her a message that I heard her. I have even had messages from people who have recently died.

But psychic experiences *scare the hell out of me*. They feel like they have the potential to be evil. They do not have the same quality of a life-changing experience for the good, as mystical experiences do.

I suppose that my first experience, when I was fifteen, the one I told you about, could have been psychic. It did carry the potential for harm, but harm was avoided.

I think it is not by mistake that most of my mystical experiences have happened in worship with grounded presences. Magic, witch-craft, spells—there is a lot of lore in other than Christian realms. These have the potential for both good and evil. Maybe that's why I try to limit involvement in psychic things. I can say no to psychic experiences. And when I say no, it usually works. Then I pray hard or go be with people.

I don't know if this is universal, but the scary stuff happens more when I am alone. I have a distinction between the mystical and psychic, but I am not sure it is shared. But for me, the distinction does feel real.

Growing up in a family where reality was manipulated, I have learned to seek external validations for what I perceive. Building in corporate checks is wise in continuing revelation. For me, validation by a larger community is always helpful.

Listening to others tell their stories can also be good because it helps me know that I have not gone off the deep-end. But I don't listen a lot, or at least not indiscriminately. Relationships develop, and I want to know that the person who is sharing a mystical experi-ence is on this planet. By "on this planet" I mean functioning in life, in the world, with their feet on the ground—still in touch with the reality I know. If they are, I accept them. But if it seems to me they are *not* on this planet, then I discount them. That which is mystical doesn't contort what we know as reality: it only adds a dimension.

I've also learned that not everything is genuine. For example, my brother once believed that God told him through the TV to go beat up someone who was interested in the woman he was interested in. To me, that was a psychotic episode; he had never had mystical experiences.

My tests for discerning mysticism from mental illness include the following: If the experience is of God, it generates good. Violence is not good; peace is. A true mystical experience engenders peace, love, authenticity, and creativity. I also look at how the person is functioning in other areas of life. The whole package should feel right.

The concept of *consolations* has been appropriately applied to mystical experiences. If it is a *consolation,* life is rightly ordered. This also applies to discernment. Someone just starting their own professional career might think that I was crazy to quit my profession at age forty to enter an unpaid ministry. My decision-making process is different, yet my ministry is a *consolation* to me and is confirmed by others. If a person is working in *consolation,* gifts are brought forth. And I have a better sense of the gift when there is inner peace than if I am anxious and spiritually off-center.

When our lives are off balance, our experience is often more psychiatric than spiritual. It is the mind coping with life. I'm not saying that we have to be perfect. God can be present even in anxiety. Under conviction, a person can be brought low, can be anxious, can wrestle in the night—but when we are open to God's presence, even in the bleakest of nights, there can be a sense of consolation. It is when we are off-balance and caught in ourselves that there is no reprieve, no reassurance.

My experiences are important, personal, intimate. So I am very careful about sharing them. I speak about them only to trusted, loved people who know me well or people who I sense may have shared a similar experience.

Sometimes I regret the sharing. One guy took it upon himself to interpret and suggested that I move into developing my psychic gifts—he did not distinguish the mystical and the psychic. Yet the responses of others have been helpful.

I never feel a compulsion to tell someone, but it is nice to be able to share. I have never sensed that experiences like these should be secret.

Over the years, Susanna has struggled with some experiences that were very frightening at the time. She has come to clarity for herself about which experiences have a positive effect on her life and which do not. She knows what she can accept in the experiences of others and what she cannot—and why. She has also learned how to ask for the help that she needs in the discernment process. Corporate validation along with an inner sense of "consolation" leads her to the clarity that she seeks.

Susanna has heard the call to ministry, continues in the waiting, and wrestles with what form the ministry might take. In one sense, her birthing has come to fruition, and in another sense, it has just begun, for when one opens oneself to the unknown, the journey is never over.

Through their wrestling with God, Marjie and Susanna have come to understandings of their experiences that work for them. Although their understandings are different from each other—and different from my own—they have been strengthened and empowered by the insights that they have gained.

I must say that in my own wrestling, I have experienced both consolations and periods in which there was no consolation. I have also experienced a short period of gnawing hunger, during which I could make meaningful spiritual contact neither with God nor with others. It was a period of despair. Yet I now look back on that period of time as the greatest learning of my life. It was the time that gave me empathy, understanding, and compassion toward others because I know that while in that place of despair, one is capable of *any* behavior that promises to get one out of it.

Looking back, I ask, was God *really* not there, or was I just unable to *feel* God's presence? Did God possibly allow this to happen to me so that I could experience the contrast to the joy of life? Was it because in the contrasts within opposites that life energy is given?

What I do know is that it was those bleak days that truly changed my life, for it was only then that I became broken enough to hear the call to a new way.

Would I be experiencing the incredible joy that I now feel in life without having endured that period of wrestling and despair?

I think not.

In the next chapter, we'll look at some whose "birth labor" was even more intense but who have nevertheless emerged from the clearing with a heightened sense of ministry and purpose.

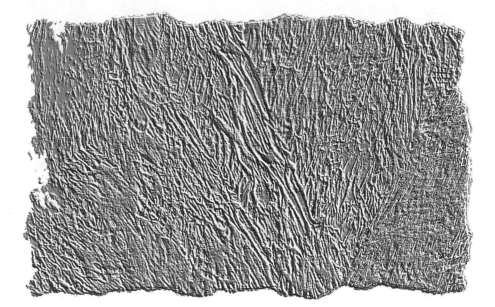

CHAPTER 7

When Assurance Emerges: Ministry and Purpose

T HE CIRCLES THROUGH which one moves in the course of one's life are seldom separate and distinct. And as I suggested in an earlier chapter, mysticism and mental illness do not always inhabit separate and finite worlds. The call that we hear may cause our lives to move through a bit of each before we emerge from the forest, before we enter the clearing, before we find the path on which we will finally walk.

But the marvelous thing is that those who hear the call, enter the clearing, and find the path of integration and wholeness have become new people. In fact, they are often richer people—so much richer that they are enabled by their experiences to minister and serve others in profoundly important ways.

I want to share three stories that illustrate in some measure what I am saying. I share the stories of these empowered women somewhat hesitantly, for some readers may be tempted to close down their ears before they hear the fullness of what these women have to say.

Let me be clear: at one time or another, all three of these women were diagnosed with clinical depression. Yet, in the end, a ministry to others emerged, a ministry that would not have been possible apart from *all* of what they have experienced.

As you reflect on their narratives, you may find yourself asking either/or type questions. You may ask, does the good that has come from their experiences of depression show that their diagnoses were wrong? Or, was what they experienced really more of a "night journey" than real depression? For me, their stories serve as yet another refutation of the whole "fine line" theory, in which mental illness and authentic mystical experiences constitute entirely separate spheres, forever separated by a line that is clear and precise.

The concept of "clinical depression" comes from a psychological context. The concept of a "dark night journey" comes from a religious context. But when we look beneath the contexts and examine the raw experiences, the two circles often overlap. Many of the raw experiences that contribute to the label of "clinical depression" in a psychological context are the same experiences that might normally be labeled as a "night journey" in a religious context.

It's important to remember that each of us makes choices about the contexts to use in developing the stories of our lives. Often those choices reflect, at least to some degree, our own social interaction with others. We sense the contexts that others are using, and more often than not, we apply those same contexts to ourselves.

Sometimes the choices that we—and others—make reflect our understanding of the "purpose" or function of an experience. Typically, those who label certain kinds of experiences as "depression" do not seek to find any purpose in the suffering. So out of a genuine concern for an individual's well-being, they work hard to suppress it.

Others are differently inclined. They more readily see some purpose in suffering. It's not that they would seek to either cause or promote the pain of others, but when it happens, they would welcome it and learn from it rather than suppress it. These differently inclined individuals tend to see certain kinds of suffering as potentially contributing to the emergence of a person's worthwhile ministry or perhaps a better ability to work and advocate for others, either on an individual or societal level.

In our culture, most of us want to know for sure the "true nature" of any given experience. When certain kinds of experiences happen either to ourselves or to others in our community, we want to *know* whether those experiences constitute "depression" or not. But in the context of a Spirit-led life, *certainty* may not be a positive value. Sometimes ambiguity and even overlapping understandings seem closer to reality.

In her 1991 book, *Dark Night Journey,* Sandra Cronk discusses three patterns of behavior that can contribute to a label of "abnormal" by those who are unfamiliar with the call to a spiritual journey. All three show up at times in contemporary stories of mystical experiences. They include:

- ❖ ANGER, which is normal when one is experiencing outward losses;
- ❖ TERROR, which sometimes arises as one moves toward the "death" of one's old understanding of self; and
- ❖ A DISTORTED SENSE OF SELFLESSNESS, which sometimes occurs when a person's desire to "do God's will" temporarily (and I would say wrongly) leaves that person believing that he or she is to have no initiative, no preferences, no likes, no needs.

For many people, these behavioral characteristics are signs of clinical depression. But they are also elements of the "dark night journey" that many go through on their way to ministry. And they are often an important part of the mystical journey to God.

For example, acknowledging our rage and our terror is often a critical step in creating new life. It isn't easy at first, but once we begin to see more clearly, we may observe that rage and terror both begin with energy flowing into our bodies. When we name and direct that energy in violent or aggressive ways (as both nations and individuals often do), it can result in massive destruction. And when the destruction goes inward, depression results. Some people try to avoid that and are zapped with fatigue. The job of repressing such energy is great. Others, however, are able to capture that energy before it gets destructively named or directed. By capturing it, they are able to rename and redirect it. It becomes creation energy, life-giving energy. When we are able to integrate this creation energy into our lives, our lives move forward. Ministry emerges.

As you read the stories of Judith, Trish, and Marjorie, you'll notice that each lived with major depression—and each, after much waiting and wrestling, emerged into some type of ministry. Judith, Trish, and Marjorie each struggled with how to interpret and frame their experiences. In the process, each made choices. Judith responded to a call into loving relationship with another. Trish responded to a call into seminary. Marjorie responded to a call into leadership among Quakers.

The vocation and the ministry is different for each of us, but the call, the response, and the patterns that you read here are similar to those that many have experienced.

FROM FEAR TO WHOLENESS
Judith's story, a journey empowered by healing choices

In the early 1980s, I experienced a life change.

I was in the midst of upheavals with my kids, who were in their teens at the time. I was emerging from yet another relationship that was ending with divorce. There were so many unknowns. I was feeling out-of-control.

A friend who was depressed went to a conference. When she came back, her life was changed. The conference had to do with "science fiction," which I had never been drawn to. But the next time I had the opportunity, I decided to go. The conference offered yoga, meditation, high-intensity sound to awaken the *chakras,* creative dance, and rituals for healing. These were all new experiences for me—very opening experiences for me.

While doing hands-on healing with someone at the conference, I came to know deep within—not from the mind—just what that person needed. I started feeling more free inside and more expressive toward others. Perhaps because of what I experienced at the conference, the love and compassion that I was showing toward others was coming from a very centered place.

Even after I returned to the "ordinary" world, I was different. My kids asked what was going on. I was more relaxed, more loving, and more kind. They loved it! There had been a teaching at the conference that said to embrace the "shadow side" when it comes so that you can heal. I think that's what I was doing.

When I think back on it, the effects of that conference went on for a long time. I remember one time walking into a bookstore—and knowing instinctively what was in the books I would look at. Everywhere I went, I felt more compassion and caring for strangers. And I just *had* to know more about Jesus.

For a time, it seemed my whole life changed.

Then, in 1982–83, I began to be enveloped by the unknown, a "night" which seemed to penetrate every part of me. I got very afraid. As a result, the depths that I felt were as extreme as any of the heights had been. Even though I knew I wasn't mentally ill, my mind kept wondering: "Am I crazy?"

I knew of a couple at the Esalen Institute who dealt with

spiritual emergencies. I went to get info, but they weren't there. Nothing that I tried seemed to help. By 1983–84, I was in a state of confusion. I would move in and out of the shadow, holding on to my mystical experiences, not knowing where I was headed.

Sometime in 1984, the night became so deep that I became suicidal. I felt so fully the pain and anguish of the world that my own inner pain became intolerable. I thought seriously about death. The pain was just too profound.

But realizing that I had the *choice* to end my life was in itself empowering. I consciously decided not to do it. I decided that I wanted to see my kids grow up. And I decided that if I'm gonna live, I'm gonna find out what it *really* means to live.

It was as if a place had been touched inside, outside, and all around me. I felt connected to a reality that was more real than the either the lightness or the darkness that I had previously experienced. An all-knowing, all-powerful presence told me that I wasn't crazy.

At the time, I told very few people. I just didn't have words. One friend who had gone to the conference with me was helpful. Marion was matter-of-fact about it. She told me not to worry. She expressed no judgment. That was critical! My own judgment and fears were so bad that I couldn't bear the same from others.

Other friends *tried* to be supportive, but often, they didn't get it. Their blank stares made me uncomfortable, even afraid. I thought, if I go over the line, they will be "concerned" about me. I wasn't sure where that would lead, yet I couldn't explain in a way that they would understand.

So for years, I didn't talk much, other than with those who have had similar experiences. I kept quiet until I had time to integrate it, until I knew clearly that it was *not* mental illness, that I was simply being shown another place to live life.

During this time, I saw a wonderful woman psychologist. She gave me her full support and acceptance. That was crucial. She offered no diagnosis. She knew it was a spiritual experience. I don't know how the psychologist knew. But she asked questions, and she had knowledge. She knew I wasn't crazy, so I felt safe.

Both Marion and the psychologist were necessary for the positive integration of my experiences. I felt strong, and I was confident that I wasn't mentally ill, but I'm not sure I could have integrated all of this in such a positive way without the support of those two.

One day I was asking myself: What's next for me? What do I need? I felt attached and attracted, and I wanted to be back in that inner mystical place. Not long after, I saw a vision of a large place on a rolling hill with lots of people in it. I didn't know what it was. But later, when I visited a yoga and retreat center in Massachusetts, I realized it was the place I had imaged. That center became my spiritual home for ten years. A place inside me was guiding me all along.

I'm grateful for all of this because others with similar experiences are sometimes diagnosed as being nothing but mentally ill. For example, when I first came to Pendle Hill, a retreat center in the Quaker tradition, I met someone who had come for a John Calvi weekend. She listed all the things that had happened to her, and much of it was just like my own experience. But she acknowledged those experiences only briefly, elaborating at length on her diagnosis, explaining all the medications she was taking for bi-polar disorder.

How one's experiences are perceived and integrated is so important. I went through some difficult days, days when I wasn't sure what was happening. But through those experiences, my life was changed. I couldn't go back, not ever.

So many people get stuck in fear and scarcity. That could have happened to me. But I wasn't willing. Because of what I had experience, I had to know more—more of God, more of Spirit, more of what I had opened into. And now, once again, I am in love!

Judith speaks beautifully of the positive integration that became possible when she surrounded herself with healing energy and beauty at an important crossroads in her life. She describes the depths and the fear that she felt as she trekked through unknown territory, not always moving on a straightforward, linear journey but always struggling to make healing choices.

It's clear that Judith's refusal to accept a pathological label for her experiences contributed in important ways to her positive integration of those experiences. As a result of that integration, her life is no longer falling apart, and she is once again able to reach out with compassion and love to others. She can't imagine ever going back.

ARE YOU THERE, GOD?
Trish's story, a journey toward reassurance and purpose

These days, because of the dramatic experiences of my religious life, I tend to think of myself as a mystic. For me, mysticism is the direct experience of the presence of God. Usually it is just an overwhelming sense of God's presence, a totally focussed attention on the divine in which everything else drops away.

Sometimes that comes through hearing words that don't originate with me, words coming at me as "loud thoughts," a phrase coined by Gerald Priestland, an English Friend. Other times, it comes as visions, visual images that seem especially important to me. These often recur over the years. Subtle changes or new images add to their meaning.

God's word can be given in other ways, as well, though I probably wouldn't describe these other ways as mystical. Words or passages might jump out of whatever I'm reading, and they might seem especially significant. Dreams, of course, are another means of communicating divine meaning and insight.

But let me tell you how my mystical experiences began.

One Sunday, back in 1985, there was a little Quaker gathering in our town. One member lived there, and Quakers from all over were travelling to her home for a meeting.

I had been clinically depressed for some months. During that meeting, I said silently, "Are you there, God?" and God said, "Yes." After a while, I said, "What about these troubles I'm having?" and the answer was "These are the sorts of problems that can be overcome."

This experience affected me profoundly, and I spoke in the meeting, telling what had happened. The fact that I had spoken in meeting seemed to fix it in reality.

After that first Sunday, I continued to have mystical experiences, and in some ways these new experiences were not always comfortable. I carried this initial experience around with me for many months, not knowing what to make of it, or what it meant. I told a few religious friends, but they were fairly dismissive.

In time, I began to doubt my sanity. I was still extremely depressed, and I wondered if I were going mad. My psychologist told me that I wasn't, but I didn't believe her. Her simple statement that I was not crazy was not enough to reassure me. She eventually became quite angry with me, angry that I wasn't getting any better, and she refused to see me any more.

I was distraught. I eventually saw a psychiatrist, who prescribed medication to relieve the depression. He asked me if I was hearing voices; I said no. I somehow knew that what I was experiencing was *not* schizophrenia. Yet for several more years, I continued to secretly doubt my sanity. At one point, I talked with a Friend who was a psychiatrist. He tried to reassure me, but I still didn't *feel* reassured.

It was four years after all of this began that I finally spoke with a weighty Friend, who asked me: "Are the messages in the context of worship?" "Do the messages lead to good?" "What are the fruits?" This Friend's acceptance of the reality of my experience, combined with a taking-for-granted of this spiritual reality, finally broke through for me. It was the reassurance that I needed.

During the second period of depression, my marriage of twenty years broke down. One day, I was sitting in Quaker meeting for worship, contemplating the possibility of leaving my husband. I said to God, "How can I be even thinking of doing this? It's the wrong thing to do!" and a silent message came clearly: "Maybe it's not the wrong thing for you." That message gave me permission to contemplate the possibility, and after a year, I did leave the marriage. Despite the pain, this has been healthy for both of us.

One day, as I walked meditatively, I rested for a while on a wooden seat, gazing up at the bare branches of the trees against the blue sky. For a few moments I felt blissfully and totally happy. It was the first time I could recall feeling that in my entire life.

The next morning, I awoke at 4.30 A.M., and for the first time, I felt what George Fox would call "the ocean of darkness being overcome by the ocean of light." In meeting for worship that day, I ministered, and that confirmed for me that there had indeed been a profound shift. I was no longer a victim to depression.

Then, just before Easter 1995, I experienced something that I have still not fully understood: a mystical experience in which I was invited by God to get to know Jesus better. God seemed to be shaking me, asking something of me, but I didn't know what. I said, "Whatever it is, I'll do it." Then it seemed as if I heard a voice asking, "What if it's something like, 'Do you accept Jesus Christ as your Lord and Master?'" Although I didn't really know what that might mean, I said, "Yes." Sometimes I remember that the voice didn't say, "Do you accept . . . ," but rather "What if it's something like . . . ?" Perhaps I was being tested.

I have always had trouble forgiving anybody for anything. I didn't know how to do it—couldn't do it. One day, early in the fall of 1996, I went to worship. I hadn't felt God's presence close to me for a while. As we settled into worship, I felt myself surrounded and filled with the presence. Images I'd worked with over the years came back to me. I had taken a Progoff journaling course in the mid-1980s. Working with visualizations, I had pictured myself as a tiny seed or hazelnut, all clenched up with its potential locked inside. I'd also had an image of myself as a deciduous tree. While in therapy during 1993–94, I'd had a recurring image of a well inside me: sometimes filled with "living water," sometimes filled with earth.

And this particular morning, I sensed again the well within me, filled with good, fertile earth, and the seed or nut in the soil, watered by the flowing stream. It was growing large and strong and full of life. I felt wonderfully supported and loved.

After a time, what came to me was the difficulty I had had in forgiving my mother. I recalled that after I'd first experienced God's presence in 1985, I'd had a sense that my problems were the sort that can be overcome. Then I realized that my mother had lived for years with the fact that one of her children—my own sister—had died in circumstances that made my mother feel that she was responsible for the death. For a few moments, I experienced a glimpse of the anguish my mother felt. I lived that pain. Then, somewhere in the midst of that pain, I was given the gift of forgiveness. I felt at one with my mother, felt as if I had spoken with her and shared that gift. We forgave one another. It was a gift of grace.

Besides my mystical experiences, I have had what might be called psychic experiences. My aunt is a spiritualist medium, and perhaps it "runs in the family." But I choose not to follow this route, whereas she runs a spiritualist church. I do sense, however, that even though we experience them differently, we may be talking about things which arise from the same place, which is God.

Over the years, my mystical experiences have definitely become integrated into my life—and in positive ways. Because of what I have experienced, my life has changed—completely. I got well (from the depression), although it took time. And I have learned so much that is valuable. I began to go to Quaker meeting, joined a meeting, and undertook further Quaker study. I have become a person of faith, and I intend to devote my life to following God's call.

Some people may think this devotion is crazy, but I say it saved my sanity. It saved my life.

I can't say of what I have experienced has been negative. Sometimes it's been hard, but in time, there has always been a sense of having learned from it, of having become more compassionate, more wise, more understanding. I can now accept that I'm human and broken—and that's all right.

Being a Quaker has meant that I can know that I'm a sinner without feeling worthless. I realize that the purpose of my life is about a connectedness with God. I got that sense right at the start—Boom!—with the first mystical experience, where I spoke to God in meeting and got an answer.

Over time, I have become much more comfortable than I once was in talking with others about mystical experiences. Hearing others' stories has helped me move toward a growing commitment in faith. Because of that, I seem to be mixing more with people who have this kind of interest or experience. A strengthened self-esteem also helps me deal with the negative reactions from others that I still sometimes get.

Sometimes, when I hear others talk about their mystical experiences, what they say resonates with me. Other times, it just seems flaky. My internal tests are a gut sense: testing it against what other people have said in the past and whether they have turned out to be sound or not. I guess when I hear things that I'm not sure about, I'm prepared to give them some time, to see what the fruits are in a person's life. Sometimes my impression becomes more positive over time, as I see a person's commitment and steadiness.

After an important conversation with God, it took a long time before Trish felt reassured in her struggle with the cultural norms of sanity. A Friend was finally able to get through and enable her to allow the gift. Even then, she struggled with programs of "right" behavior, sometimes finding that the "right" behavior was wrong for her.

When doubts were overcome, the mystical experiences she had had became gifts for Trish. They helped her work through difficult experiences in her daily life. They encouraged her personal growth. And they enabled her to find her purpose and ministry.

Trish now describes her purpose as a connectedness with God. Boom, it was there, she says. For some, the mystical experience cuts through layers and sends a powerful message deeply and quickly. But Trish acknowledges the importance of discernment in her (and others') experiences, for she finds that the fruits are not always immediately discernable.

THE DEEPER YOU GO, THE CALMER THE WATERS
Marjorie's story, a journey toward a richer spirituality

The easiest way for me to define mysticism is through these well-known words of John Woolman:

"There is a principle which is pure, placed in the human mind, which in different places and ages hath different names; it is, however, pure and proceeds from God. It is deep and inward, confined to no forms of religion nor excluded from any where the heart stands in perfect sincerity. In whomsoever this takes root and grows, of what

nation soever, they become brethren."

Why Woolman's words speak to me will become clear when I describe the mystical experience I had in 1973 when I was twenty-eight years old. I had been attending the Anglican church for about two years, having previously thought of myself as an atheist, and had been a communicant member for six months. The vicar of the church was very much at the liberal end of the Anglican spectrum, so I was able to approach my new-found faith with surprisingly little dogmatic baggage.

Besides the witness of the vicar himself, the major influences on my faith at the time were the Sermon on the Mount and a book of prayers by Michel Quoist called *Prayers of Life*. For me, the emphasis in both was on living a Christian life rather than on accepting a particular dogma. And that was good, because I was too much of a skeptical scientist to go so far as to literally believe virgin births or physical resurrections.

All of this was perfectly acceptable to the vicar, and I took my calling very seriously. In fact, this commitment I had to living a Christian life is still the only explanation I have for God taking the initiative and giving me a mystical experience.

It happened over a period of about four days, during which I was somehow taken up into the mysteries of the universe. I cannot remember any details now, as I wrote nothing down, but I know that the essence of the mysteries was paradoxical in nature. I felt connected to a benevolent power that is hard to express in words. It just was. I have never experienced anything like it since, but this one experience was sufficient to determine my life thereafter.

At one point I had a clear sense of my humility being tested like Jesus was tested in the wilderness. I felt that, had I wanted to, I could easily win the lottery—but I chose not to. It sounds crazy, but I really felt it. Also, during the experience I received what I call two "intimations" from God.

The first of these intimations came in words that absolutely threw me. A voice, both external and internal, said, "Hello. You made it. Which way did you come?" I was shocked enough at experiencing what I assumed to be God without the addition of this revelation that suggested that there are different paths to the same experience. At this time, my knowledge of other religions was absolutely zilch. I followed up by checking out the intimation for myself, engaging in an extensive study of other faiths as well as the lives of many mystics and creative people. As a result, I can now say as John Woolman does, that I know experientially the truth of what I heard.

There are people that I read—or meet personally—who also know this deep, inward place. And as Woolman says, we are brethren. For me, it is the presence of this connection in the deep that defines or rather confirms the mystical dimension. It is a heart thing. Maybe this explains why some of us are touched by certain experiences and some are not.

The second intimation was equally unexpected. It concerned cancer. The intimation was that cancer was not an illness in the same way as other illnesses, for cancer has an external cause. The intimation was that cancer had to do with our state of being, and thus we had it in our power to heal ourselves from within. Again, I was amazed, and at the time, I thought this a very strange idea. This was years before I heard anything of alternative medicine or holistic healing. In fact, I was flabbergasted when I first heard about such approaches. I still have no idea *why* I should have received this, other than that I might have made connection with the collective unconscious, which is part of Jungian theory .

There is more. Some two months later, I fell into a very strange depression. I say strange because I had suffered from depression five years earlier, and this was of a different quality. With hindsight, I understood the earlier depression as a reaction to difficult external circumstances. But the second had no obvious cause at all. In fact, given the profound mystical experience I had just had, there seemed no reason for depression at all. This made what I was feeling extremely hard to comprehend. My biggest fear was that I was going mad.

Then, after about three weeks, I had an amazing dream. In the dream I was being offered the "kingdom of heaven." It was clear to me that if I accepted, I would die. Beautiful and tempting as the offer was, I chose to refuse it. Instead, I felt called to stay in the world in order to help others find God.

The next day, the depression had completely gone, leaving me feeling as if I now had a deep connection with the death and resurrection of Jesus—not literally, of course, but experientially. I would describe it as an archetypal experience.

Some years later, when I was studying Buddhism, I came across the phenomenon of the Bodhisattva, and this almost blew me away. Bodhisattvas are beings who refuse Nirvana in order to help everyone achieve enlightenment. The similarity with my dream experience was uncanny.

Long before any of this happened, back in 1967, actually, I began a science teaching career—which ended abruptly with a nervous breakdown and a suicide attempt. I like to think that I had completely recovered from that difficult time and that my later mystical experiences were entirely what they purported to be. But I cannot deny that the nervous breakdown happened—and could be relevant. My only other experience that could possibly be connected with some type of mental illness was in 1991 when, in the course of deep psychotherapy relating to the death of my father and other losses, I did a Summer School on Creativity, during which my unconscious became too open and I felt as though I was flooded with light. I have still to put meaning on that experience.

As far as talking with others about my mystical encounters is concerned, it has often been very negative. My husband was around through all of this, but sadly, he has always been reluctant to talk about it, even now when he knows how important it is to me. I suspect it frightens him a bit, and his main response at the time was relief when I was back on a more even keel.

I shared some of it early on with both my father and my elder brother, both of whom I wanted desperately to be understanding and supportive. In fact, it was my father who had suggested that I buy *Prayers of Life,* one of the books that became so important to me. But they couldn't accept it. My brother rationalized the whole thing as a chemical imbalance in my brain.

I felt quite shattered by their response. That cause me to take the whole experience underground. It was far too precious and important to me to allow it to be battered.

I wanted to put what I had experienced into some kind of meaningful context. So eventually I set about my own private quest for understanding.

Six years later, I risked sharing it again, this time with a very evangelical Christian. Her response was to suggest that I must have been so sinful that God had to go to extraordinary lengths to get me sorted out. But this didn't quite square with the fact that I was a fairly ordinary sort of person whose worst crime was maybe taking a little bit of loose change out of my father's pockets to buy cigarettes when I was about fourteen.

So back the experiences went, deep inside myself, out of harm's way.

It wasn't until 1986, at a weekend course at Woodbrooke College, after I had become a Quaker, that I shared it with John Punshon. His response was appreciative and accepting, the opposite of what I had found anywhere else. In fact, he suggested that I write about it for *Friends Quarterly*. I felt really affirmed by his response, but I didn't have the courage to go public with it.

Since then I have shared it from time to time. At first, it would have to be when I felt *really* safe. These days, I have less fear. Yet it is still too precious to take the risk of being mocked in any way. I have a deep fear of it being reduced somehow to mental illness, because it would invalidate so much of my life if that were true.

Along the way, two very differing explanations have been offered for my experiences:

1) kundalini rising, which is a Hindu term for a vital force that lies dormant within a person but when activated can lead an individual toward a deeper level of spiritual power, or

2) an unfortunate slip into psychosis.

The second explanation freaked me out at the time, and my therapist was horrified at this turn of phrase from someone in a place of authority at a training institute.

This is not comfortable stuff! Even now, I share it apprehensively—and only because I hope that it will lead to oceans of compassion for those of us (and there are *many* of us) who are carrying this sort of stuff around.

The whole business of madness has scared me for years, and I truly do believe that, at this point in time, I *am* sane, whatever that means.

Not only do I call myself sane, but I call myself a mystic, and rightly so, because what I have described definitely felt like a direct, unmediated experience of God. Having a direct relationship with God—and living in a way that is in keeping with that context— remains the most important thing in my life.

Incidentally, when I talk about being a mystic, I am not talking about psychic experiences, at least not as they are usually understood. My definition of mystical experience is fairly specific, and it would exclude any experiences that were simply about predicting the future or were simply concerned with "things" out there.

For me, the mystical embraces both the immanence and transcendence of the divine in a non-dualistic and paradoxically mysterious way. However, to a certain extent, it depends on the definition you adopt. It is very tricky precisely because it is hard translating experience into categories.

Once I had had the mystical experience, I could never get it out of my mind. I began reading religious books avidly. They were mostly Christian at first, and with hindsight, I think I might have become a stereotypical born-again Christian had it not been for the intimation that mystical experience of the kind I had is not to be confined to one religion. I still find the usual interpretation of the passage in John where Jesus says, "I am the way, the truth and the life; no one comes to the Father except by me," totally incompatible with what God seemingly revealed to me. And in the course of my degree studies, I found resonances of my experience in a wide variety of places: not just within other faiths, but also in poetry, music, art, even science.

The environment of these deeps is just as Woolman says it is, and it saddens me so much to see the disharmony that proliferates at the surface, especially among those people of faith who feel they have a monopoly on truth and belittle other faith paths.

In 1982, I was clear about all this—and feeling very alone. My revelation seemed to fly straight in the face of an immense Christian bureaucracy that would have Jesus as the only way to God, and the whole thing just felt too huge for me. I despaired of finding a community of people for whom all this was meaningful and accept-able.

Then one glorious day I read *Introduction to Quakers* by George Gorman, who was then secretary of Quaker Home Service. It came in a free pack of information that I received about the Society of Friends. From what I read, I concluded that there were at least some within this religious group who felt as I did. Maybe that's why becoming a Quaker felt so much like coming home.

As luck would have it, the first Quaker who befriended me after that was a dear seventy-four-year-old woman who belonged to the Quaker Universalist Group. Two years later, I was accepted into membership on an overtly universalist ticket.

Since then, my spirituality has grown and blossomed. My greatest joy has been service for the last nine years as an elder in Britain Yearly Meeting. I care passionately about the right holding of meeting for worship, because at its gathered best, it reaches those same beautiful depths which feed the cause of love.

The vigorous debate between Universalist and Christocentric Friends profoundly saddens me. But the conflict is like a stormy sea. And in a stormy sea, the deeper you go, the calmer the water becomes. If I have a purpose now in relation to all of this, I think it is in searching for ways to encourage that depth, ways to encourage others to experience that calm. Of course, I still struggle at times to overcome my fear and lack of courage in following through on all this.

I find that when others speak of their mystical experiences— their encounters with that depth—my response is primarily related to how I resonate with the person concerned. It's a felt thing. Deep meets deep, and it is usually clear when I am in the presence of something "more than." I sense a shift in the quality of the moment.

For me, when a Quaker meeting is truly gathered and spoken ministry comes out of the depth of a presence, I am caught up into it. And when being caught up doesn't happen, my sense is that the ministry may have involved a very erudite and loving thought, but it has come from the letter and not from the spirit.

That being said, it also may be true at times that I am not gathered enough in myself to resonate, but I try to be very disciplined in meeting for worship—precisely because I care about gatheredness. And I find that the feeling, when it happens, transcends content. I have been caught up in the presence of what others have shared, even when my mind, on its own, might have been skeptical.

Marjorie shares her struggles with depression and doubt, letting us see the incredible journey she has undertaken, a journey from the pain of the night to life in the Light. The difference in the quality of life possible after the rising, as compared to her life before the plunge, is truly noteworthy. What a gift!

I pray that in many life situations, all of us would remember Marjorie's metaphor: that the deeper we go into the waters of a stormy sea, the calmer those waters will be. Marjorie experienced some serious storms, but in the quiet depths, she was opened to divine mysteries and holy intimations that have left her with precious gifts to share.

Judith, Trish, and Marjorie all experienced a diagnosis of depression. Seemingly, those diagnoses were appropriate. All three experienced as well what Sandra Cronk calls a "dark night journey," a journey during which they encountered mystical openings, found purpose in their suffering, and followed new leadings into productive ministries. After hearing a call in the midst of a long and difficult struggle, they entered a clearing and, empowered by what they had experienced and supported by those who understood, they chose the path of integration and wholeness, a path that allowed them to serve and minister to others in a richer and more meaningful way.

For people like Judith, Trish, and Marjorie, what they have been through is perhaps hinted at in words like these:

I spiral downwards.
Into the pit.
A lid closes.
I am there.

Forever?
So it seems.

A ladder emerges.
I climb up.
I fall off.
Again.
And again.
I fall.

One day.
A helping hand, pulling.
I don't fall back.
I am led forth.
A new path.
Mine.

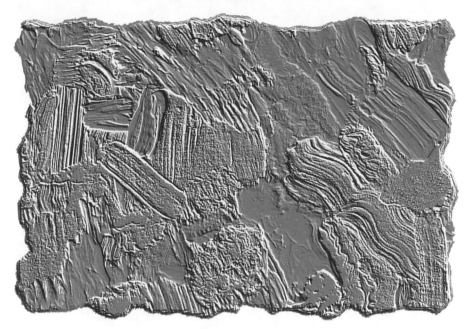

CHAPTER 8

"When we give a problem to God, God gives the problem back to us, along with new ways of dealing with it . . ."

Hospitalization and the Healing Presence

M*EANWHILE SAUL, STILL breathing threats and murder against the disciples of the Lord, went to the high priest and asked him for letters to the synagogues at Damascus, so that if he found any who belonged to the Way, whether men or women, men or women, he might bring them bound to Jerusalem. Now as he was going along and approaching Damascus, suddenly a from heaven flashed around him. He fell to the ground and heard a voice saying to him, "Saul, Saul, why do you persecute me?" He asked, "Who are you Lord?" The reply came, "I am Jesus, whom you are persecuting. But get up and enter the city, and you will be told what to do."*

Acts 9:1–6, NEW REVISED STANDARD VERSION

According to the Book of Acts, the man named Saul, who later became Paul, had visions. He heard voices. He had also been caught up in plots and violence against others. How would he have fared in our culture? Would people have been afraid of him? Would he have gone jail, been institutionalized, had court-ordered counseling, or maybe been put on antipsychotic medication? How would he have been treated when people became afraid of him?

Many people today are being contained in ways that lead to suppression of their gifts. Many people are being labeled "crazy" simply because in some way or another they are feared.

What follows are the stories of women who have had experiences of God that they would label mystical—as well as experiences that they would call mental illness. They have shared these stories to educate others of us who want to know how to better accompany those who are having the kind of spiritual experiences that can lead to crises.

It is my hope that nothing that I say in this book or in this chapter will in any way dishonor the good work of psychiatrists. That isn't my intention. It's true, however, that some of those with whom I spoke while undertaking this research felt that their encounters with psychiatry were either negative or mixed in effect. Yet others felt that they had been labeled and medicated in ways that were genuinely helpful.

It's important to remember psychiatry's positive potential for those who have mystical experiences. In such situations, the psychiatrist/client relationship works best when the psychiatrist can respect the spiritual experiences of the person. Many good things can happen when a psychiatrist and a client are well-matched, with an agreed-upon boundary between what is acceptable and unacceptable. None of us should assume, however, that there is one single boundary that is "right" for everyone or that works for all. A psychiatrist and a client need to agree on what that boundary is in their situation and work toward keeping that boundary clear.

When it comes to psychiatry, the stories in this chapter lie on a continuum. Jean considered her experiences with psychiatry to be negative. Mariellen, on the other hand, found psychiatry helpful. Jane initially had difficulty, then moved into an experience with psychiatry that was helpful, as did Annie. But as you will see, all four of these women have found it helpful to have people who can faithfully accompany them on their journey.

KUNDALINI AWAKENING
Jean's story, an example of a negative experience of psychiatry

In 1984, at the age of 46, I was opened to experiences that I had no prior concept of.

The changes in my body were perceptual, visual, auditory, and olfactory. These transient perceptual changes occurred when my body, although physically still, was experiencing tremendous energy. Every cell felt highly charged and aware.

Visually, I had the ability to see detail on a mountainside at a distance of a mile as if I had high-powered binoculars. This could last five to eight minutes. Walking into a store, I could see a glow around all the clerks and customers. Time, as I had known it, sometimes seemed suspended, and I would feel as if I were in another dimension. I could hear sounds and occasional words and knew these were occurring in this other dimension. At one time, I seemed to be part of historical events, such as the crucifixion or the holocaust, all of which seemed to be taking place in the present moment. At times, I enjoyed the smells of sweet perfumes, freshly baked chocolate chip cookies, or baby powder, and these smells would be present even when they had no outer explanation.

There were also thought process changes, changes in feelings, and behavioral changes. I was experiencing tremendous love and power for which I had no preparation or explanation. I also had a new and strong sense of inner guidance that gave me the strength to accept what was happening to me. I saw it as an adventure—and an unfolding story. I had feelings of love and compassion for everyone and everything in the world. A desire to do no harm was strong. I was unable to watch or read about violence in any form. If I did, my whole being reacted as if the violence were occurring to me. The popular media—television, newspapers, movies, books—repeatedly affected me in adverse ways. I could sometimes skim the newspaper, but I had to be careful that the words I was reading did not get to the feeling level. If they did, my body would experience waves of anxiety and panic.

The explanation that fits my experience is the "Kundalini awakening" that is commonly described in the Hindu tradition. Early Christians referred to it as the Holy Spirit or the Holy Terror because of its unpredictable effects. The process leading to the quickening of this energy has been understood by mystery religions through the ages and has been the goal of yogic practices.

Signs of the Kundalini awakening include involuntary shaking or "quaking," high-energy episodes along with unusual sights and sounds, profound moments of bliss, out-of-body experiences, and new psychic abilities. Although these events can be extremely intense, many people are able to accept and eventually integrate them into their lives. Others are frightened and either try to forget or, in an attempt to find help through the medical system, become labeled and treated as one of the "mentally ill."

My husband (ex-husband now) was a medical doctor, and he was able to listen to my experiences for a couple of days. Since the only understanding he had of such events was in his psychiatric training, he felt I was experiencing some type of mental illness. At the urging of a colleague, he persuaded me to see a psychiatrist. I knew I was having a spiritual experience. But as a nurse myself, and thus a part of the medical establishment, a I knew there was no way I could convince anyone of this.

My inner guidance continued to be strong and loving, and I felt no fear as I was admitted to a psychiatric unit for a ten-day period. During my stay I did not speak of my experiences, knowing that if I did, I would be there for a longer time. My children, relatives, and friends for the most part tried to ignore what was happening, although their concern for me was evident.

There was no evidence of support from others for what I was experiencing. While hospitalized, a psychiatrist told me "not to get involved with areas like that." This was never explained or elaborated, but I suppose he meant the occult, of which I knew nothing. The psychiatrist put me on medication that caused me great distress. I had no psychotherapy, and there were no religious or spiritual resources available.

I was able to cope with the changes because of the sense of a loving guidance and support within myself that was the source of my strength. I managed to get through difficult times by taking one minute at a time and not looking too far ahead to the future.

My inner guide let me know some of the healing therapies that I needed. I needed to dance. I needed to read books and articles with a spiritual theme. And I needed to be outdoors. I also became aware of where I could find explanations for what had happened to me. Nothing that health-care professionals offered was helpful, but these other things were.

The kind of environment that is helpful to someone who is going through a spiritual crisis is one in which a person can share what is happening without judgment on the part of the listener. When we know that another is respecting our experience, it is easier to accept suggestions, such as the need for sleep and food during high-energy episodes.

My inner guide led me to books and groups of people who have had similar experiences. Health-care professionals do not understand these experiences. So they need to take a learning perspective rather than seeing themselves as experts. They would be less likely to do harm if they would listen to and respect the experience.

Helpful programs include nutrition, dance, art, writing, body therapies (such as massage), and constructive explanations for what is happening to the body and why. Yoga is sometimes helpful for this.

Over time, I have learned to think of myself as more than a physical body with a consciousness. My new awareness is that I am consciousness, inhabiting a physical body for a time. I look upon myself and others as students who are here on earth to learn. Our ways of learning are different, but opportunities individually designed come to all of us. I hold relationships more lightly than in the past. Problems that people have are for them to solve. I listen to others so that they are able to hear themselves better.

The National Mental Health Consumers Association, located in both Canada and the United States, is organized and administered by former consumers of the mental-health system. They understand the dilemma we face. This group is aware of the number of people being labeled mentally ill who are having spiritual-emergence experiences. After having been labeled as mentally ill—and having been offered no positive understanding of their experiences—many people simply spend the rest of their lives managing medication in an attempt to suppress their experiences, and that's tragic.

I appreciate Jean's story because she has given such a clear description of what was helpful—and not helpful—during a very intense period of her life. In describing her experience as a "kundalini awakening," she appropriates a framework used by Hindu practitioners. Others with whom I spoke also found this framework a helpful way of defining and understanding their experience.

In reflecting on Jean's experience, it seems clear to me that our culture is generally not well prepared to be of help to people who are having such strong energies come into their lives. And the medical community sometimes imposes its own frame of reference even when that frame of reference is not helpful. Jean's words are a reminder to me that many times we need to be more in a learning mode than in an expert mode when it comes to dealing with others' intense spiritual experiences.

FRIENDLY ASPECTS
Mariellen's story, an example of finding help in the midst of illness

I define mysticism as an attitude of listening for God's guidance and direction. Of course, some people assume that when God speaks, it will inevitably be accompanied by a dramatic, twenty-one-gun salute. In reality, God usually speaks to us in the midst of our ordinary lives. We encounter God's direction and guidance through personal insights, through prayers in the Spirit, through reading spiritual books, and through cultivating friendships with other spiritually minded people.

I am fifty-six years old, and over the years I have had two kinds of spiritual experiences. I have had experiences of the living God working in my ordinary life. And I have had experiences caused by my mental illness, experiences in which I carried on long conversations with God, Jesus, the Holy Spirit, and occasionally the Virgin Mary.

Let me give you some examples of what I regard as the real thing when it comes to experiencing God's direction and guidance.

On a recent Sunday, I went into a meeting for worship, asking that a former friend apologize to me so that I could stop being angry with him. But during meeting, I found myself remembering a time when, as a college student, I had worked in a men's prison. I had been warned not to fraternize with prisoners. Usually we four women in the office walked over to the officers' mess to eat lunch, but one day there had been a freezing rain, and we phoned a request that prisoners bring our lunch to us. As we ate, I thought about the two young men in thin cotton coats who had brought lunch and were waiting to carry the dishes back through the sleet to the officers' mess. I took a paper towel, scrawled "Thanks!" on it, and then drew four smiley faces. I propped the note against our dishes as the four of us were leaving the lunch area. None of us thought anything about it. But one of the prisoners later smuggled a note in the lunch boxes to an older woman in the office, and when he was caught, he told about my note. The older woman—instead of me—got in trouble. Someone at the prison asked me if I knew about the note. Being struck by a kind of fear-amnesia, I denied any knowledge of the note I had written. It took a year after I left the prison before I came out of my fear-amnesia and remembered the note I had written.

And as I sat in the silence of that meeting for worship, I wondered why I was recalling that old lie. Was I supposed to share it in meeting? It seemed not. And then the Spirit moved: "Did you ever apologize to anyone for that lie? Can you understand the fear-amnesia that caused your old friend to lie to you? Can you forgive him now, even without an apology?" And so, there in the meeting, I forgave that old wrong. If God could forgive *my* lie, then surely I could forgive my friend's lie. It was a powerful meeting for worship—and a totally silent one.

For the most part, I have discovered that God generally speaks within my mind. What usually happens is that I recite my litany of woe—and a thought comes to me. Often that thought is a seed that I have to think about a long time before the insight comes. Sometimes the thought is a question that sheds a whole new perspective on my dilemma. Sometimes the thought is a comment on my dilemma. Whatever form it takes, it is a fresh outlook that is beyond my immediate powers to assimilate. It takes time for me to digest a God-message. It always gives me a wider view of the issue. Over time, I have come to associate God with getting me out of my poor thinking, and I find myself turning to God for direction more often.

When we give a problem to God, God gives the problem back to us, along with new ways of dealing with it. A necessary step that I had to take was to learn how not to live by my feelings. A saying that helped me many times was, "Don't be an emotional reaction: be a person." Through many mistakes, I have learned to acknowledge my feelings while doing the right thing anyway.

I think it was part of God's purpose to teach me to do as much as I could for myself before turning to God for help. These days, I try to think carefully about issues. Then I pray to be given more understanding. I seek human counsel about the right thing to do, and I pray to understand more about what *I* am to do. Then, when I think I understand what is called for in the situation, I pray to be enabled to do the right thing. When I make mistakes, I pray to be able to learn from them. I do as much as I can for myself, and then I ask God for the specific help I need at each step. With God's help, I have learned to be a person instead of an emotional reaction.

I think it was part of God's purpose to make me feel my feelings to the very core of my being—and then let them go. When I let go of a negative feeling, it no longer has power over me. Many times, God has challenged me to replace negative feelings with more positive ones. With God's help, I decide on a more positive response to an old issue, and then I ask God to help me choose the new way. My issues have been complex, so I have had to let go of many destructive emotions. Many times, once I was ready to let go, I still needed God's help to actually release these deep-set feelings.

Today, I'm still mentally ill, but my behavior is a great deal less sick now. I've let go of feelings that caused me to hallucinate, with the result that now I seldom hallucinate.

Many times I felt like I was going crazy, especially when I would consult God, Jesus, the Holy Spirit, *and* the Virgin Mary—getting four completely different views of what I should do about a situation. That's definitely crazy-making.

Usually, in the beginning, when I started hallucinating, the voices said wonderful things. Sometimes they even gave me some insight into things. But after a day or two of listening to these voices, they would became extremely punishing and scary. Unlike many people who hallucinate, my voices are alluring to start with and only become something to fear later on. So I have learned a sort of intellectual fear that sometimes has helped me keep from cultivating the voices.

Three years ago, I began having two kinds of voices: the old crazy-making ones, and other voices that I thought were trying to help me make sense of what I was experiencing. The new voices were extremely fallible, and they occasionally got frustrated with me and punished me. Yet often they *were* helpful. On one occasion, when I had been hallucinating having sex with God, one of the voices broke in and asked a helpful question that made it possible for me to figure out what it was in me that brought on the sex-with-God experiences, and eventually I was able to release that negativity in me.

Since then, only once in three years have I had conversations with God in which God answers. Since that time during which I released a number of negativities, I have learned to understand the voices in me as being entirely internal to me. For me, the voices are of two types. They are either an internalized tape of someone important to me in the past, or they are my unconscious mind, whom I call "Friendly Aspects" and with whom I have now negotiated a peace settlement.

Fear has been a major part of these experiences. I was quite fearful about these voices I was hearing. Then some of them began making sense and helping me with the other voices.

Several things helped me deal with the fear. The first was my sense that I was struggling with my illness in the presence of God. This whole three-year struggle, in which so many of the old fears have been set aside, was initiated by a prayer in the Spirit, in which I was given the words and the concepts to ask God for help.

I have found that when we pray in the Spirit, words and concepts come that move us forward in our spiritual journey. Sometimes a prayer even becomes its own answer. For many years I was unable to pray without hallucinating long conversations with God. Ironically, my faith deepened as a consequence of the inability to pray. I felt that without prayer I was walking blind through life, yet I came to sense God guiding me in that blindness. I felt sorely deprived without prayer. Yet one night as I lay in bed, I prayed with all my heart: "God, I know you are with me every step of the way in this life without prayer. Life is rich and full, and I am growing in the Spirit. I know that, and I am grateful. But I liken my relationship to you with my relationship to my husband. I know that I need to *do* love, and I work hard at *doing* my love for you. But one of the joys of my relationship to John is that I can *tell* him that I love him. Please, I'd like to tell you that I love you." I hallucinated again afterwards, but I knew I had prayed in the Spirit. I knew I had been heard. And I believed God had promised me that I would pray again.

When the new voices began appearing shortly after I had prayed this prayer, I simply remembered the prayer, prayed for guidance, and began trying to think my way out of the illness. In a sense, I went *into* the illness to gain control over it.

Of course, there have been many mistakes along the way. My counselor—God love her—urged me on many occasions not to listen to the voices for fear that I would be sucked in by them. I did make many mistakes, but once I had prayed that prayer, I sought God's guidance at every step of the way, believing that God would not have given me that prayer unless God truly wanted to help me with my illness.

Another thing that helped to lessen my fear was the recognition that slowly, step by step, I was releasing the negativities that had caused many aspects of my illness. Whenever a new issue presented itself for me, a new issue that I needed to face, I would grab hold of my courage and say, "God is trying to help me. God has a strategy that I'm beginning to recognize in all of this. I will *cooperate* with God."

Fortunately, I ultimately found a few people with whom I could talk about these experiences. My counselor wisely told me that she herself had no expertise in spiritual matters. And I knew that none of the people to whom I had turned for guidance during the previous seventeen years of my illness would be trustworthy in dealing with the positive events of the last three years. So I asked my Quaker meeting to appoint a "committee of care" for me. I helped choose the people I needed on that committee: two young Friends who were into Wicca and an elderly gentleman who had advised me on dealing with spirits a time or two earlier. I asked the committee to pray for me daily and meet with me on a regular basis for worship and discerning. The elderly gentleman had a discussion with the one spirit that I had not been able to get to leave by offering to pray for him; that spirit was vastly irritated, but it did leave me at the gentleman's direction. After that, the committee helped me discern how to deal with the voices that were internal to me.

Do I call myself a mystic? I do. I believe that God does give people direction in their lives. I believe that in my case, God often has to be silent and subtle, but God sees to it that I get the direction and help that I need. God doesn't speak to me in a voice: that would only confuse me about where reality is. But God does see that I get the direction I pray for.

Even some of the difficult struggles that I have had seem to me to be a part of the mystical experience in the sense that I believe God put those negativities in the world to teach people not to act out on their feelings. And when those negativities have taught us what they are there to teach, they willingly leave. Well, mostly they leave willingly. One negativity wanted to stay and punched me so hard that I was sick for a couple of days, but he apologized, by the way.

I think it may be the case that some negativities are *not* working for God, but the ones I dealt with definitely were. The negativities themselves were not God. But they worked for God by making me feel my feelings to the very core of my being—so that I would ask God to help me release them.

I don't think that God works directly with all people in the same way. The negativities that I dealt with are only one of God's tools. I have had experiences with ESP after meeting for worship, and I think that for some people, ESP may sometimes be among the tools that God uses, but God is bigger than ESP.

My experiences have transformed not only my life but also my understanding of the purpose of my life. I have learned that God wants me to behave as if I'm sane—and share my story of living with mental illness. Although there has been no complete healing in my case, I believe that I am to give hope and help to other sufferers of mental illness who are troubled by sexual spirits. I am to show others that it is possible to live sanely in the midst of mental illness. I have learned that it is possible to have a rich and full life living in the presence of God in spite of mental illness. I am living evidence that being mentally ill does not mean that one is necessarily sinning.

I have heard other people in meeting share their mystical experiences. And I have sometimes read about such experiences in publications like *Friends Journal*. My main test for whether something is sickness or health is whether a person's life has been or is being changed in positive ways. In other words, I tell the tree by its fruits. I have grave doubts when I read stories of people's experiences and see that they have made no concrete changes in themselves as a result of those experiences.

Everyone's journey is different. Mariellen says that she has "negotiated a peace settlement" with "Friendly Aspects." She has learned to deal with "negativities," and she sees that learning as a gift that brings her closer to God.

Mariellen has done the work necessary to create a clear sense of boundary for herself. There have been mystics across the ages who have used very sexual language to describe their unitive experiences with God. But for Mariellen, the idea of "sex with God" is unacceptable, and she has found an understanding and a boundary that suits her.

She shares the struggle with her "mental illness" and describes her growing sense of being in the presence of God. Although she says that she has not had "complete healing," she has a strong sense of God's help, God's direction, God's guidance. Like others, she has had difficulty finding the kind of help that she needed. Fortunately, she now has a good match with a psychiatrist, and the committee of care within her meeting has proven very helpful. Mariellen shares concrete examples of the ways in which she sees God working in her life.

LET THE HEALING BE COMPLETE
Jane's story, an example of struggling with past traumas

For me, mysticism is a searching for direct guidance from God, not mediated through any other person or through Scripture.

I myself have had mystical experiences while in Quaker meeting. One was close to the "white hot center" of meeting. I don't know what the question was, but I remembering answering, "OK, I'll do it—but this time let the healing be complete!"

That was a *sacred moment*. At the time, I had no memory of abuse. But it emerged, and it was overwhelming. There were intense consequences to my praying this prayer for complete healing. When I said, "Let it be complete," I was asking for a depth that I had no idea of.

That sacred, God-given moment had consequences. The work that I needed to do started. I was in crisis for about three years, but that crisis was part of the healing. Even when I didn't feel the Spirit, I knew it was there. I don't think I could have done it without the Spirit, without medical intervention, without poetry, and without

(F/f)riends. I was fortunate that resources were provided. The process is on-going.

I am forty-four years old, and I was diagnosed in 1991 as having bi-polar disorder. That was during a twenty-three-day hospitalization that followed a forty-eight-hour psychotic episode with spiritual content. Prior to the episode, I had experienced a great deal of stress caring for my mother, who had cancer.

The trigger for bi-polar disorder went from baseline to psychotic in forty-eight hours or less. The break happened on a Wednesday night. I slept, and then I spent the next day psychotic. My husband and son left for the day. My delusion was that I was to arrange universal peace. I ritually rearranged the furniture in the house to create patterns. Then my husband and son came home. I couldn't stop. I couldn't even eat. I kept trying to create patterns. I got very "not gentle." I attacked the police when they came. I was obsessed with reconciling opposites. This was not like me.

The poem by William Yeats called "The Second Coming" was very important: "What rough beast slouches . . ." I was seeing that rough beast in the emergency room. My husband and son say a lot happened that I don't remember.

I was given antipsychotic drugs, and I slept, but much of that time is not clear in my memory. I do remember that my psychiatrist was very respectful of my spiritual beliefs. The delusion was like a dream: the content just came to me. Other patients have had more shattering experiences, including encounters with the Devil.

For me, all of this was very unpleasant. I do not like being psychotic. Parts of those days had great beauty. I had acceleration of thought, and I wrote a lot. I wrote things like, "How do you unknot?" Much of what I wrote was lyrical, but it was also psychotic.

I know it was psychotic because when I look back, I say, "That was not normal." But when I was going through it, it was very real. The episode was quite damaging to my concentration, and it still takes a while to reorganize.

I was not diagnosed until age thirty-eight, and my illness was not well-controlled until recently. When I was taken off my medications, I got manic. My version of bi-polar involves more depression than mania. I thought I could cure it by will, but I could not.

They tried other drugs for a while. I am now on lithium. I don't think the lithium has interfered with my spirituality and creativity, and I like that. I've had six months of stability. It's unfolding.

Part the illness has to do with my past history, and part is biochemical. Healing couldn't happen without the biological part coming into place. On the other hand, the healing that I asked for was not a healing of biochemistry but a healing of heart, of spirit, of psyche.

God can be a pill sometimes—and I mean that in *both* ways!

When I realized the severity of my condition, I was enraged; it didn't seem fair. On the other hand, although I haven't worked in the lab since my psychotic episode, I do have a Ph.D. in pharmocology. Maybe that makes me more open to gifts that come through medication.

I've been married since 1989. I met my husband at a meeting for worship. We dated for seven years before we were married. He's a psychiatrist. And in the course of all that I've been through, I developed a lot of anger toward psychiatry. But being with him and seeing the vulnerabilities of psychiatrists has helped me heal my anger toward the profession.

Fear is still a problem. I am often afraid of ordinary things. I don't know why. I don't drive. I am terrified of cars and have never had a driver's license. My sister is also fearful, but she has learned to drive.

Until my psychotic break, I was never afraid at meeting for worship. Then I started experiencing terror in meeting for worship. I was flooded when I went in. I don't know why. I still don't know what I was afraid of. So now I am trying some new things in some new environments. For example, I decided to spend some time at Pendle Hill, a Quaker retreat center. That took a lot because I don't usually travel on my own. I had never caught a commuter train before, and yet I had to take one to get to Pendle Hill. I was really scared, but I did it.

Ordinary fears are exaggerated for me. For instance, I get terrified when people are late. I have fears for my son. He has learning disabilities and is trying to get a college education. Maybe it is a vague fear of being hurt. I think these may be leftover terrors from when I was very young and neglected.

For years, until I began getting my body back, I never felt hungry, no matter how much I did or didn't eat. When I was little, being fed was not consistent. Maybe that's why I literally did not know what the sense of hunger was. It would have been too terrible. I didn't learn it until one day when I ate something—and noticed that a certain feeling went away. I finally understand how my husband can come home and say he is hungry. Until recently, I couldn't feel it. So I assumed he couldn't either.

Lots of terror has been working its way to the surface. For

example, I recently had an experience not of remembering but actually re-experiencing being three and being held by my neck and being hit against the door. In re-experiencing my life as a child, I thought, "When I get big, I'm gonna kill her!" And I *was* angry enough to kill her.

When I called a friend and told her, she said, "Good work." She meant that I had pain and terror locked inside me since those early years, back in infancy. It needed healing, and once it was out of the box, it had a life of its own. So it had to be dealt with. It reminds me of the scar that I have on my arm, a memory of my arm being cut by my mom to teach me not to break glass. Living with that scar is not a choice that I make. It's just there.

In seeking a healing that is complete, I have been strengthened by many examples and many gifts. And those gifts have been given by both Quakers and non-Quakers.

When I first heard Jane talk about her "illness" as a part of her healing toward wholeness, I was baffled. But since talking with Jane, I have heard many others use similar language. Often, in the midst of such statements, I find myself wondering why we call it an "illness" when it is clearly part of a healing process. In response to those wonderings, I have been given the analogy of a fever, an intense condition which functions in the body as part of the healing process. Jane shares her struggle with "the fever" so poignantly!

Like others, she struggled to find the help she needed. She came to find peace with the psychiatric profession by seeing empathetically the vulnerabilities of its practitioners, vulnerabilities which they are often reluctant to let us see.

The search to live a rich life with God while bearing the terrors of early trauma is a combination that often sends people into difficult times. But Jane, like so many others with whom I have listened, believes that the freedom that comes with healing is worth the pain that marks the struggle.

CLEARING THE WAY FOR A NEW SELF
Annie's story, an example of finding Light in even the bleakest hours

I have five years' worth of stories related to mysticism and mental illness. Yet I have seldom had any place to talk about these experiences that feels really safe.

At one point, when I was "in difficult straits," I turned to a teacher and friend. for help. Without even knowing all of the details, she helped see me through some horrendous experiences.

You see, as a child I was called Annie—and I remained that child long into my adulthood. Not too many people knew, for I managed myself very well. I built a successful career and an authentic faith on the foundation of a child. But that foundation was not strong enough to stand up under the stress of increasingly demanding jobs, and in my last job, as a corporate trainer, I broke down. In the midst of that breakdown, I recovered trauma memories from my childhood, and I also had two experiences that I call mystical.

What I didn't realize at the time was that I *had* to break. I had a very controlling, rigid, and unconscious ego that clung to an idealized self-image. I believed I was a loving, mature Christian. And so it took three psychotic episodes and numerous hospitalizations to level that old self. (By *psychotic,* I mean being "swamped by my unconscious.")

The destruction was hellacious. Instead of holding to the daily routines that make life sane, I abandoned myself to my inner world. That world was populated not only by my own clear thinking but also by other "voices," some familiar, some not. The voices led me to do things outrageous and frightening. Once they led me into an abandoned cabin in my neighborhood where I lost myself in an imaginary world of goblin faces on the wall. That was what I chose to do instead of waiting patiently for the bus that would have taken me to my therapy appointment that day.

This was my mental illness—and it was devastating. I was incapable of telling anyone except one dear spiritual friend what I was doing. The craziness served its purpose though. It cleared the way for a new self to grow, a self capable of setting boundaries, speaking the truth, and discerning the light.

People ask me, "What enabled you to keep going? How did you get through?" I respond, "By sheer will-power and by grace." The will-power had to come from within, but the grace came in the form of that spiritual friend, who never stopped loving me and trusting that the Light was at work, even in my bleakest hours.

Jean, Mariellen, Jane, and Annie worked hard to survive having their lives totally disrupted. They sought—and found—purpose in their extreme suffering. In time, all four of these women connected with the help that they needed to reconstruct their lives. And the new lives that they have built are even richer and more centered in God than their previous lives. All four now have people around them to help hold and "contain" the intense feelings and out-of-the-ordinary experiences that they struggle to integrate into their lives.

In the next chapter, we will explore more fully some of the ways that each of us can help others build the kind of containers that are needed to better integrate some of the most difficult—and enriching—experiences of our lives.

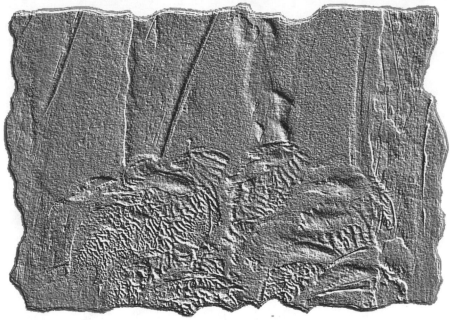

CHAPTER 9

"The activity of the Spirit is like lava flowing under the surface of the earth, and on occasion, as in volcanos, there is a great eruption of Spirit energy . . ."

Finding Containers for the Spirit's Energies

*T*HE INFINITE EMPTINESS *of the human heart is first experienced as terror. When we are content to wait, it is transformed into an eager emptiness waiting to be filled. Paradoxically, this formlessness needs an outer structure in which to rest if it is to be used creatively. Mere formlessness points to a destructive nihilism. The mystery is, as it were, a jewel that needs a setting.*

Alan W. Jones in JOURNEY INTO CHRIST

As Alan W. Jones suggests, the "jewels" that emerge from our experiences often need to be placed into a context. And from what I heard as I undertook this research, it's clear to me that many people who are experiencing a pull into the spiritual "journey into Christ" are longing for a "setting" into which this jewel can be placed.

Participants in this project often spoke of their desire for a safe place to be and a safe place to share one's experiences of God. Many names were used for this safe place, but numerous times participants referred to their need for a safe "container."

In this chapter, you'll find several people talking about what has been helpful to them in building containers, as it were, to hold their spiritual experiences. Quaker meetings have played important roles for all of them. Participants have benefited from prayer, worship, spiritual friendships, clearness committees, oversight processes, inspirational writings, accountability, and support. Trained professionals have also been helpful in building containers, especially when such professionals are able to meet the mystical traveler with respect, honesty, and a freedom from judgmentalism.

I began this project by asking, "Why is it that the same set of experiences can sometimes be labeled as mystical and at other times be labeled as mental illness?" Since the same kinds of experiences can evoke two different interpretations, the answer to my question didn't seem to lie in the actual content of the experiences. What has become clear to me, however, is that at least part of the answer lies in this matter of containment.

At a recent Quaker meeting, a Friend ministered, saying that the activity of the Spirit is like lava flowing under the surface of the earth, and on occasion, as in volcanos, there is a great eruption of Spirit energy. In dramatic fashion, a power that was hidden suddenly becomes visible. Although I don't want to imply that all activity of the Spirit is like a volcano, the metaphor does seem fitting. Certainly there are people for whom Spirit energy comes like nothing short of a volcanic eruption.

I realize that I'm mixing metaphors here, but this same ministering Friend suggested that when an eruption occurs, the receiver of that energy is like a fish in an ocean. A fish needs the unconstricted freedom and safety of the water as an organic container to hold it and provide for it. Of course, not all of us are fish, either literally or figuratively. So in each life, the most appropriate container must be carefully discerned, for at different times and in different places, different creatures need very different kinds of containers. A fish, for example, cannot breathe if it is not in the water. But other creatures cannot breathe at all if they are forced into the water.

While there is no fixed pattern for the containers that all of us sometimes need in our lives, it's clear that constructive containers allow space for the individual to breathe, while simultaneously providing a structure that is strong enough to hold whatever needs to be contained.

Over the years, many kinds of containers have appeared in my life. Recently I came downstairs to find June, the Friend with whom I live, cleaning out cabinets in the kitchen. On the counter were many containers: small ones, large ones, clear ones, pink ones, blue ones, flat ones, tall ones, containers with lids and others with no lids. The image remains like a photo in my mind: there were more kinds of containers available than I could have ever imagined.

In our lives we also have many kinds of containers. We have containers within ourselves. Our own hearts, bodies, and souls can serve as containers. For many of us, our writing and our art work serves in this way. Then there are our families, our friends, the groups that we belong to, our faith communities, and sometimes we even have professional therapy containers. Containers come in so many forms that I cannot even begin to list them all.

In my own spiritual life—and in my own experience of "seismic activity"—a variety of containers have been helpful. In using such containers, I have learned some things. First, I have learned that I benefit from having not just one but many containers in my life. No single container could possibly hold as much energy as has come to me. Second, I have learned that there is a container within myself. My own heart, soul, and body hold much spiritual energy.

I also use images. One of my most important images is of my soul as holding God-energy for the purpose of co-creating and co-directing my life. Another strong image for me is an image of Jesus beside me, providing comfort.

Recently, I was given a powerful image of my heart becoming like an egg and cracking, opening up. I could see my hands emerging, at first like a newborn, shaky and having a hard time standing on my own. The image reminded me of a newborn calf or colt on my family's farm. At first, it can hardly stand, but within a few hours, it can walk, and before long, it can run and play. I painted my hands emerging in four paintings that came from these images. In the second painting, my hands are turned inward and I am looking at them in wonder. In the third, they turn outward again and are holding a huge block of gold. In the fourth painting, they are extremely strong hands going into the world powerfully. The images came and were powerful visual symbols for changes happening in my life. The beauty was incredible and the pain excruciating and clean; it felt redemptive.

This visual image is an example of the kind of inward experience that can happen when one's "seismic activity" is in motion. I am incredibly blessed because there are many people in my life with whom I can share such an experience, knowing that they will appreciate the beauty and growth that are symbolized by the image that has been given to me. Their appreciation for what I was able to share touches on something else that I have learned: sometimes I need humans to accompany me. Sometimes others need to be a part of my container. Sometimes others need to help provide the "setting" for the jewels that I experience.

Consider the image that I was given of an egg with hands emerging. The energy and the pain that came with the experience were clearly to be felt and not modified or changed. I knew it to be redemptive pain. I have come to distinguish pain that needs to be changed from pain that needs to be felt, even though that is not a distinction usually made in our culture. Our culture tells us that all pain is bad. I know differently. All pain hurts, but some leads to positive changes, and I believe that, with faith, most all of it can be transformed to good. The clean pain of the heart egg cracking open was clearly to be felt and not changed. It felt like the pain of the birthing process.

After the experience, I needed to share it with others. It had more energy than I could hold in myself. But how—and with whom?

I have many people in my life who can enjoy the jewel—and provide the setting. I feel deep gratitude for them. But who are they and how did I find them? I found them by simply sharing my experiences and discovering who was receptive. I have shared the egg image with many people, and now I share it with you. My hope is that you can receive the sharing in the same way that the people close to me have received it.

There is a choice that we make about how to receive. Some hear the story and hear pathology; to some, no matter how I describe the beauty of the changes in my life, if they hear that there was pain involved, their response is, "Poor you." But "poor you" is not a helpful response. To some, no matter how redemptively I describe the pain, they will suggest medication to suppress it. That, too, is not helpful. There are times for sympathy and for medication, but when a person is having a powerful, beautiful, life-changing experience of God, that may not be what is most helpful.

But the most unhelpful response of all is judgment. I use *judgment* in the sense of condemnation or belittlement. We all must make assessments in our daily life. For example, if someone had been in my presence while I was feeling this pain, they might have thought I was having a heart attack and taken me to the hospital. Somehow we must make a distinction between assessments about valuable and helpful actions with our friends and those actions that create pathology where there is none.

Doubt and fear are contagious. If someone responds to me with a framework for my experience that is not mine, it can start to create doubt and fear. This is especially true with experiences such as the one I described, because in the psychiatric world, there are many who would describe such an experience as "hallucination," "mania," or "psychosis." When it comes to pathological labels, there is an abundance of choices. As a professional, it seems to me that there have been too many times when I and others have used our roles as assessors to pathologize and judge, when that was not helpful to the person having the experience.

Thinking again about the responses that have been offered to the image of the cracking egg and emerging hands, the response that was most helpful to me came at a conference for mystics. I shared the image that had been given to me. Afterwards, in the simplest sort of way, someone said, "That is very cool. Let me know if you need anything from me when you are trying to understand and integrate that image. By the way, would you like to display your paintings and tell your story? I know of an art show that is coming up that may have space."

There are many Friends—and friends—with whom I can talk and share in spiritual friendship. I have had numerous clearness committees, and I still have oversight committees for my projects. I attend prayer and healing groups. I have individuals who value my work—and say so. Most important is a safe place for worship. Among Quakers I find the structures for providing the capacity for holding my spiritual work.

In my own "seismic" experiences, my chosen profession has been somewhat less helpful. Although he did not know how to deal with spiritual content, I was nevertheless fortunate to consult a therapist who assured me that I was *not* going crazy—and I was never labeled with a mental illness. Beyond that, help has come from the writings of classical saints and mystics. People trying to live a life committed to God—or who can respect my desire to do so—have likewise been helpful.

Deciding with whom to share such a precious experience is crucial. An ancient writer on the experiences of mystics, an individual who used the name Dionysius but who is now generally referred to as Pseudodionysius, argued against sharing one's experiences with the "uninitiated." Likewise, in the Gospels, there is a warning against casting your "pearls before swine" (Matthew 7:6).

My experience of the heart egg cracking open was definitely a pearl. Not to share such a pearl seems arrogant. Yet I also understand the concerns of Matthew and Pseudodionysius, for harm can come to people when spiritual experiences are shared without some care and discernment. In deciding to share these experiences with a broad audience in the pages of this book, I had to have faith in the strength of my container. Much faith is required.

The image of the container also reminds me of a concept presented at a 1994 conference sponsored by the "Foundation for Community Encouragement." During the conference, we who attended were presented with the concept of a "jug" as a container for a community. An important goal was to make the "jug" big enough and strong enough to hold as much as possible of each of the members in the community. Perhaps, with God's guidance, I have built a container for myself that is strong enough to hold what I need held—and that is an important definition of the word *community* for me.

For those whose life includes mystical journeys, the purpose of a "safe container" is to help them integrate their experiences of God in a way that makes their life richer. In the pages that follow, several participants speak about the containment of their experiences and about their times of talking and listening to others.

Jane, Mariellen, and Helene told parts of their stories in earlier chapters. As you may remember, all have been through crises and at one time or another, all have been diagnosed as having a mental illness. They have unique stories, but each has important lessons to share on what was helpful and what was not when their spiritual experiences moved into a crisis situation. Jane and Mariellen, for example, found both Quaker meetings and psychiatric interventions helpful for them. They speak to the particulars of their coming to find the help that they needed—and offer some good advice for professionals who seek to help others in similar situations.

Accompaniers from Quaker meetings have often told me that it is easier to help someone who is open about what is happening—and clear about what is needed. Unfortunately, shame often clouds one's capacity to be both open and clear. Helene avoided that pitfall. She was open with her meeting, and as you will see, she offers concrete suggestions about how to ask for what is needed. While she believes that sharing one's experiences is crucial, she finds it equally important to discern one's own best way of doing that sharing.

You'll also hear from a woman that I call Annie. She, too, has much to teach us.

A SAFE AND GENTLE PLACE
Jane's search for a container to hold and support her experience

I saw my psychiatrist for six years. He was always gentle and respectful. My spiritual life was honored. In my family tree, there are five generations of mental illness. I had worked with excellent therapists before, but they gave me no medication. The disease gets worse if it is not treated with medication. Some are opposed to medication, but manic psychotic episodes are no way to live.

In the course of all this, I did intensive work with my Quaker meeting. I had a clearness committee until I moved. After working with the healer John Calvi, I got better.

The role of the clearness committee was listening, clarifying, reflecting back, and holding me in prayer. They did not assign things, but they did suggest things. For example, although I am not much of a Scripture person, they suggested Scriptures from the Gospels that were helpful. For a while, my husband was living in a different city, and during that time they were a special resource. A lot of my psychological work came in meeting for worship.

My criteria for deciding whether I would talk to someone about my experiences includes an assessment of the other person's ability to understand. There are cues. There are people who believe that there is more in heaven and earth that first appears. I'm talking about those who believe in Spirit and soul, even when they cannot be captured in an electron microscope. I am one of those who believes in souls as well as electron microscopes!

I will share with any who are able to listen. Of course, some can't listen. My mother is incapable of listening. She makes everything mean what *she* means, and what you mean is lost.

My meeting went through all of this with me. When memories of abuse came back, I called someone in my meeting. Then I stood in meeting and said, "Hold me in the Light." It seemed like it was not just my will that made it happen. There were never secrets, and that was critical to my healing. Others shared deeply their own experiences in efforts to help me.

I just recently switched psychiatrists. The new one is older. I talked about prayer with him and acknowledged that there is no proof of prayer. He said, "Oh, yes there is." So I am again working with someone who can respect my spiritual journey.

To find a good psychiatrist, I asked colleagues for references, and my husband (who is a psychiatrist) helped discern. If I didn't know someone who is a psychiatrist, it would be harder. I might go see a couple of people. Then ask your heart. If you don't feel they are right, they are not right.

The qualities of the psychiatrist that are most helpful to me are these:

1) I need someone who is gentle.

2) I need someone who is honest. Honesty is key. I don't trust easily. It's a slow process. Without honesty, it's impossible.

3) I need someone who will respect me.

Maybe it would help if I gave you an example of healing in the psychiatric setting and healing in the spiritual setting. I learned to tell my psychiatrist when I was angry with him. Because I was angry, I thought he would know I was angry. He didn't necessarily. So he taught me to express things. He also taught me about boundaries. If others felt anger, I thought I too had to feel it. I learned I didn't.

In the spiritual setting, I worked with a healer three times. The first time was when I came to Pendle Hill in 1992 to work with John Calvi. I was in terrible shape: depressed, suicidal, trapped, and in an ungodly amount of pain. I took a look at John and my soul said, "What took you so long to get in my life?" I cried for one-and-a-half days. It was good.

Everything was locked inside and couldn't get out. John had me put my feet on a chair. When he put his hand by my knee, it was like a knife went through my knee. John just said, "It's bad." I felt relief. "No wonder I feel bad, it's bad," I thought. The rest of the week was amazing. I was feeling parts of my leg that were suddenly alive for the first time. I remember that at the meeting for healing, I noticed that my two legs were on different wave lengths. He held me and guided me and I was able to surrender to the Spirit. There was immense healing. I was in the center of a pillar of light. I can't tell you what was healed because I don't know what it was. I am not afraid of John like I am many others.

Later I talked to my psychiatrist about the experience with John. His focus was to try to gain understanding rather than judging. That felt good.

While I can talk with many people about my experiences, there are some I don't talk with. I won't talk with a friend who is a physician and was my husband's roommate in medical school. Phil is fact-oriented, concrete. I like him, but he would not understand. I am not ashamed, but there is no way to talk about it that he would understand. Nor will I talk to those who are excessively judgmental. I don't just mean about myself. I don't talk to them about the weather, either.

In addition to being bi-polar, I had an aberrant upbringing. My mom was not capable of being a mother. I lost memories. Pain and memories came in meeting, sometimes even physical pain. Once an axe was buried in my head. As awful as it was, meeting was the safest and most gentle place for that material to unfold.

I was very public. The meeting knew what was going on. One member sat by me and offered to leave with me if it got out-of-control. If I had not had the Quaker meeting, my fear would have been uncontrollable.

As I have said before, I don't think I could have done it without the Spirit, without medical intervention, without poetry, and without friends and Friends.

WHEN WAY OPENS
Mariellen's search for a container to hold and support her experience

Some of the things that people did for me were wonderful. For example, the times of worship together with my committee of care were extremely helpful. I often was enabled by worship to reveal a delusion that I otherwise would have hidden, even from the committee.

The committee also helped me by negotiating with the voices external to me, persuading them to go and be in the presence of God, then holding a communion service to celebrate their decision to do so.

An elderly gentleman had advised me earlier how to negotiate with the spirits for myself. He said to treat them with the same gentleness and firmness that I would a human who was causing me harm. He taught me to offer to pray for a spirit and taught me the form that a prayer for a spirit could take.

A friend that I consulted before the committee was formed advised me to release a negativity by making affirmations and guided me a couple of times on the phone how to do so. After the spirits left and I was dealing only with voices internal to me, the committee gave me the concept of negotiating with and praying for two aspects of myself, the Internalized Young Man and the "Friendly Aspects." This latter prayer helped me solidify the belief that my remaining voices were internal to me, and that understanding helped me grapple with my delusions and obsessions as feelings that needed to be faced.

One of the most helpful things was offered by a woman who had also experienced sexual spirits. She accepted my word that that was what I was dealing with, and she gave me a very useful bit of counsel. She said that relationships with sexual spirits are almost always highly codependent. On occasion thereafter, she advised me on ways to step firmly outside the codependency triangle of Victim, Rescuer, and Victimizer. This person is now an ex-officio member of my committee of care.

Some things were not helpful. For instance, the voices that I was experiencing eventually began making a kind of sense for me. And at that point, all of the kind, wonderful, and otherwise helpful people who told me not to cultivate the voices were simply not being helpful. For one thing, by that time, the voices wouldn't have left me alone. Once into the experience, there were only two options. I could tell my doctor—and take massive doses of medication. Or I could walk through the valley of the shadow and slowly sort out the issues that were causing me to hear voices.

My first psychiatrist, when I told him that I had talked with Jesus, declared firmly, "Jesus doesn't talk to people." I thought, "You're full of it." I knew that I *was* spiritually ill, but he lied to me, and I didn't trust him after that. By the way, that was the shrink who had a large portrait of himself hanging over his desk. He left town rather suddenly when a woman patient filed a suit saying he had raped her. He had a reputation for giving female patients a pelvic exam upon entry into the hospital. He never tried to come on to me. I guess I just lack sex appeal!

My second psychiatrist and I worked together very well on most occasions, possibly because I didn't talk about my spiritual problems with him. On one occasion, when I was very sick with medication problems, I told him that I had spent the whole night in a Quaker meeting. He knew enough about Quakerism to tell me that what I was doing was not a Quaker meeting. That was true, but it wasn't helpful.

What he should have asked was, "Why are you spending the night in meeting?" I would have told him that I was losing my grip on reality and was using silent worship to try to regain control. Then we could have worked on the real problem. Instead, we used polite words about what constitutes a Quaker meeting. The guy was deeply humane and also never hesitated to call things the way he saw them. I liked him. We are still friends. But I didn't willingly talk spiritual things with him.

My present psychiatrist and I have never discussed spiritual things. Neither of us volunteers thoughts on the subject. We work together very well, and I have a lot of respect for my current shrink. I suspect that he knew I was working on hard issues during the last three years, and he did his best to help me keep the medications low enough so that I could think. This counselor, as I said, states clearly that she is not qualified to talk about spiritual matters.

I have found some ministers to be helpful. It was a minister to whom I talked about my fear that my voices were spirits possessing me. I told him that the spirits left me, hovered over me a few minutes, then reentered me. "They wouldn't let me go," I told him fearfully, and he responded, "Who won't let who go?" That gave me something to think about. It took eight years for me to finally let go of "the guys," but he had given me the clue that I had the final say in the matter.

I went for a time to a Bible study led by a lay minister. When I told her I couldn't pray because it made me hallucinate, she told me firmly that I was listening to the devil. I thought to myself, I should try to educate her a bit about mental illness, and I wrote her a carefully thought-through letter. She wrote back to tell me that I must obey God's wishes. She indicated that I must pray in order to do God's wishes, and if it made me hallucinate, I was being sinful. I stopped going to her Bible studies. Later, I saw a newspaper account saying that that particular denomination was actually a cult, and that several people in town were in counseling after going to the church.

My friend Steve and I exchanged many letters while he was in prison. I call him my minister-felon because he was exceedingly helpful with many aspects of my spiritual illness. He applied common sense to my problems, and I learned a great deal about healthy spirituality from him. When I wrote a year ago to share with him how it happened that I finally released the spirits within me, he simply urged me to be very careful and promised to pray for me. I knew he would have deep reservations about the approach I had taken to help myself, but I also wanted him to know how it happened that I am so much better. And he was right, I did need to continue to be careful.

Several factors contributed in positive ways to the integration process. A 12-Step organization for mental sufferers called GROW was very helpful. It gave me the basic idea that my hallucinations were expressions of feelings, and it taught me better ways of managing my feelings. Basically, what GROW taught me was to behave as if I'm sane. The jargon for this is to "not act out on my feelings." I was in GROW for six years, and for four years I was the leader of my group. Not acting out on my feelings got a lot of practice while I was leading a group of eight maladjusted people!

Another factor that helped in the integration was that I became convinced that God didn't want me to pray, because prayer brought on hallucinations. So for eight years, I didn't pray, and instead I used

Hannah Whitall Smith's methods to discern God's direction in my life. Her book is called *The Christian's Secret to a Happy Life*. Her five methods of determining God's will are:

1) Checking Scripture. Hannah Whitall Smith doesn't say how this should be done. Some people find help by opening the Bible at random and reading the first passage that the eye falls on. I have tried this a few times and found it unproductive for me. My aim is to someday know the Bible so thoroughly that the passage I need will naturally occur to me, and that works sometimes. In this learning stage, I consider it no coincidence that the helpful passage is often in the very chapter that I read during my Bible study time.

2) Checking Common Sense. I call this "behaving as if I were sane." It's my primary weapon against insanity, because if I behave sanely by doing the right thing in spite of clamoring feelings, it helps to keep the feelings from taking over next time. By continually choosing to do the right thing and ignoring my feelings, I can keep the mental illness backed into a corner where it does less harm. Figuring out what sanity calls for in a given situation is helpful in my case because I had good common sense before I became ill. I try to remember what I would have thought in a similar situation before the illness struck. But while I was learning how to behave as if I were sane, I depended very heavily on the next method.

3) Checking with Weighty Friends. In the beginning, I built up a cadre of five thoughtful people, each of them deeply committed to helping me think through my issues without pushing a pet solution on me. When I mulled over a problem, I often found myself feeling moved to ask my friends for their ideas. Sometimes I consulted all of them, but usually I consulted one or two, trying to spread the load of responsibility more or less evenly. I told them that I was trying to spread the grief around. Often my friends didn't agree among themselves about what I should do, and I tried to think about the reasons for their differing suggestions. Usually their reasons were sound, and helped me think of the best solution for me. Weighing the conflicting suggestions of reasonable people helped me build confidence in my own common sense again. For several years, I was able to get along with just occasional check-ins with someone. A few years ago, my illness entered a new phase, and I have been meeting regularly with a committee of care from my meeting. We have worshipped together and discerned in broad outline what I should do. Between meetings, the members of the committee have prayed for me every night. The love of my friends has supported me. Bless them all for being there!

4) Checking Reality. If I feel the Spirit is moving me along a certain path, I have learned first to take one step and assess its results. If I'm still not sure, I can take another small step to see whether Way opens.

5) Paying Attention to the Stops. If I feel any stop, I have learned not to move on the leading until the stop is removed and I feel clearness.

I've been working with these guidelines for a number of years now, and have a few observations that may help others. In the first place, I make mistakes all the time in this process of discerning God's will. I try to learn from my mistakes. Often my mistakes occur because I give in to a feeling, so I try to examine the feeling and then ask God to help me deal with it. God works with me and, over time, my feelings have become more manageable.

In the second place, God usually doesn't tell me what to do, although there have been exceptions. Mostly, God gives me insight into a situation and leaves it up to me to consider prayerfully the new information and decide what to do. I try to listen carefully for any stops before I act.

In the third place, sometimes I discern carefully and find clearness to act, and yet my action totally bombs. If I rethink and conclude that the Spirit was right the first time, I have learned to think over the reasons for the failure and ask for further insight. This cycle of checking reality, asking for insight, reflecting on it, and prayerfully acting may be repeated many times before a complex and deep-rooted problem can find resolution. Some people may call this learning through trial and error, but I prefer to think that sometimes God teaches me through successive approximations. God gives me as much truth as I can chew at any one time. Then God gives me more understanding. So when a problem seems intractable, I have learned to have faith in the process. I persist in listening for guidance and praying for help in becoming God's person.

Finally, we very seldom are given to know God's plan for our lives—not going in, anyway. Sometimes we are given the vision to see very dimly only half a step ahead—a full step ahead is in total darkness. Yet if we put our hand in God's and take the step, and then another and another, checking our leadings at every step, we will be able to look back someday and see God's vision for us more clearly. And when we are given to know God's vision, it will be one of drawing us into a closer walk with God. Getting God's work done, yes, the work is important. But mostly it's about having a relationship with God.

Hannah's guidelines helped me find my way to God without

prayer. And when the new voices came to me after the prayer in the Spirit that I mentioned earlier, I knew it was time to trust God implicitly and behave as if I were sane while I went into the illness to learn how to let it go.

One of the things that helped me the most to avoid prayer for those eight years was a discussion I had with the minister named Roger. When I told Roger of my decision not to pray, despite my feeling that not praying separated me from God, he looked reflective. Then he compared my relationship with God to the relationship of a small child to a father. The father hears a cry in the night and knows the child needs to go to the bathroom. He goes and gets the child and carries it to the bathroom, the child does his business, and the father carries the child back to bed and tucks it in. The child usually never wakes up, yet he trusts that the father will take care of his need. That image of being carried like a child stayed with me through those eight years of not praying.

CONNECTING WITH BOTH OTHERS AND SELF
Helene's search for a container to hold and support her experience

In seeking containers for my experience, I found a psychologist who was helpful. With that psychologist, I released a lot of energy by talking and crying. But the professionals that I encountered in the hospital were not helpful. Well,there was one woman who was compassionate. I was putting out good energy—and receiving good energy. That was reassuring. But what was really helpful were those people outside the hospital who were holding me in their prayers. That sounds simple, but it was very helpful.

If any of this happens again, I'd talk more about it. I'd go to someone to help me process it. I would want to be in my own house. I need space to contain it.

I would say the same to others who are having an emergency in their spiritual lives. It is important to be close to others during that time. You need people to help you be aware of your humanness. You need a hand to hold—someone who is calm. You need reassurance, and you need grounding in ordinary things—daily rituals, mundane life. You need something around you that reminds you of who you are, something comfortable, something day-to-day. In addition, those around you need to know that what you are going through is difficult and they need to treat it with respect. It may not make sense, but have respect and faith in the person! My mother had faith in me no matter what, and that was tremendously important.

Since those days, I have had a powerful dream in which a friend said, "Go to God." I said, "Well, take me to it," and she said, "No, if you think I can do that, you don't get it." The dream was a reminder to me that others can help and give comfort, but there is an aspect of our journey that each of us is uniquely responsible for. In the future, I will not look to others to help me make sense of what is happening. I must make sense of the experience within myself. Yes, I would like to *share* it with others, but not as a necessary way of making sense out of it.

Insanity is an invention of the individual's failure to have a place in society. It is also a product of isolation and despair. Humans need to feel that certain aspects of their reality are shared with others. It's the same for mystical experience. Having a forum for looking through the individual vocabularies and metaphors would help spiritual seekers see their journeys in relationship to others.

I needed my own space to come down. It was important to have my own room, a place to write. It was important to write and have the option to connect to the outside world, in my own time. I also had art supplies. That was important. I had some familiar things around me. I knew how to create that space, and they let me.

I had to write in order to process what was happening. It was an erratic, riddle-kind of poetry. I was making sense of something that didn't make any sense. I was turning ideas into good ideas. I was dealing with fear. I felt ill, and writing the symptoms helped me let go of them.

SEEKING HELPERS, NOT RESCUERS
Annie's search for a container to hold and support her experience

Initially, I ran into a lot of problems caused by my own confusion over the word *ego*. I wasn't sure if it was healthy or unhealthy. Now I think it can be both.

I define *healthy* ego as one's capacity to act in the world, to set boundaries, to identify needs and meet those needs. We all need egos. I define *unhealthy* ego as "small" ego. It's that part of ourselves that acts from self-will, from fear, from pride. It wants its own way. Mental health requires that one hold onto a *healthy* ego, while mystical experience requires that one let go of *unhealthy* ego.

What opened me to mystical experience was my capacity to let go of unhealthy ego. However, I went too far and began letting go of healthy ego as well. I was abandoning normal ego functioning and assuming that God should be directing my daily life through a constant flow of "signs."

The biggest problem I had during my experiences was containing them. Before my breakdown, I was totally unaware of the importance of containers. That was because I always had one. Prior to 1992, my life was well contained. I belonged to Christian community. I had a good job, a close circle of friends, active participation in 12-Step programs. I had a spiritual director and a therapist. I just took those things for granted. So I never realized that for my life to work, I needed a strong container.

Early in my life, I had perhaps been too well defended. For years I had been busy trying to open things up in my life. By the time of my breakdown, I was very open. I had good access to material that had been buried for years. So at that point I needed to make a shift. The issue was not opening up more material but simply working with and containing what was now conscious. However, I never made that shift, at least not for years. And that was where I got myself in the most trouble.

Had I realized that a strong container was the most essential element in weathering a breakdown, I would have known to stay put in Baltimore, instead of leaving to go on retreat. By going away on retreat, I lost the container I so desperately needed. And despite the fact that I went to an intentional community, it is difficult to build a new container when in crisis.

To build a container, one must first know how critical it is. That's where images or actual holding and playing with containers of different sorts can be the most help in developing that knowledge. No one ever did that with me. But, boy, do I wish they had! Take a plastic bag and fill it with water. The water is contained, held, so it doesn't leak. Other people don't get wet. One doesn't lose what is of value, which is the water. But what happens if the plastic bag is punctured, or is placed near a radiator? Uh-oh, problems.

So let's move from plastic bags to human lives. Psychic material is like precious water. It needs to be held safely so it can be processed, resolved, and learned from. And the sturdier the container, the safer it is. So maybe one would want to put the plastic bag inside a waterproof box. Then it couldn't be punctured so easily. Or maybe you just need heavier plastic. For me, the parallels are helpful.

So how did I create a safe container? By thinking about what needed to be held, for how long, under what circumstances. Then I tried to identify the available sources for containment. Those would be both self-generated, such as a journal, and other-generated, such as a spiritual director or therapist. Creating safe containers includes considering the physical environment (both during the day and at night), other people (personal and professional), activities, institutions, communities, and small groups. A good match between what needs to be contained and the container is important.

When I chose to go on retreat, I knew I needed a safe place. However, I chose an inappropriate container. What needed to be contained was trauma memories, not spiritual experiences. So a day hospital for trauma or abuse survivors would have been more appropriate than a retreat. That would have given me a suitable substitute for my home container—a daily structure to replace the work structure that I had just lost.

Someone else can play a pivotal role in helping someone who is on a new journey understand the necessity of containing the experience—and then build a container. Sometimes even the relationship between a helper and an experiencer can be the beginning of a container. The experiencer may for the first time have a safe place to talk about what he or she is experiencing. In talking about the experience, we actually begin to contain it. We are drawing boundaries and applying descriptions.

In a letter sent to me the year after I left retreat, a friend wrote that the critical issue facing me was "finding the right kind of help." I didn't realize it at the time, but how right he was! After years of struggle because I didn't have the right help, I know now that this is the critical issue.

Just as with containers, different kinds of help are appropriate at different times. First of all, one must be willing to seek out and receive help. That is the first hurdle. The second hurdle is figuring out whom to ask for help. I was fairly willing to seek out help. I had done that for years, ever since high school when I first sought out a Christian who could help me discover my own sense of faith.

There is a difference, however, between seeking help and seeking to be rescued. A friend gave me this analogy: Suppose I have a dog, but I don't know how to take care of it. I go to a friend to ask for help. I am not asking my friend to take care of the dog for me. I am simply asking my friend to "help" me take care of it. So helpers are teachers. They eventually work themselves out of a job.

I ran into problems early on in my crisis because, out of my desperation, I stopped looking for help and started looking to be rescued. That was when I stopped listening to my own inner wisdom and started looking for people to tell me what to do. It was understandable. I was terrified and full of distrust, particularly of myself. I knew that I was in worse shape than I had ever been and that I needed more help than I had ever needed before. However, I did not need to be rescued. I was still an adult who had not yet turned over responsibility for her life to someone else. I think there can come a time when one *does* need to turn over responsibility, but circumstances need to be very extreme to warrant that kind of action.

I did finally do that during my first psychotic episode, when I went to a friend, Cara, not having eaten or slept well for days. She took one look at me and said, "I'll take you to the hospital." I didn't argue. It was clear to both of us that I could no longer care for myself. Turning over responsibility to Cara and to the psychiatric unit was the appropriate thing for me to do. I hated doing that. However, I was also lucky that there was someone there to take responsibility.

Reflecting on "help," I realize it's a tough one in our culture because so much of our conditioning teaches us to do it all by ourselves. Spiritually, that is very dangerous. Help can come from books, but when you are in crisis the help most needed comes in the form of another human being. And for me at least, the depth of crisis I was in made it harder than ever to commit myself to another human being. That paradox continues to puzzle me. At the time in my life when I most needed help, I was also least able to receive it. I hope that is not true for anyone reading these words. If so, you have my deepest empathy. It is an awful place to be.

This is such a large topic, and I have had so many different helpers and have matured greatly in my capacity to know what I need and then seek out someone to meet that need. It's a huge story. So how do I condense that story into learnings and advice with examples that illustrate? Well, let me offer some guidelines for help:

First, decide what the problem is that you need help with. Use both your own inner wisdom and feedback from your immediate and most trusted community, which is to say, personal friends and professionals. If you need relief from some kind of distress, you first need to identify what the distress is. In the medical model, diagnosis must precede treatment. I've never been a medical-model person, but it does have its usefulness.

Second, once you know what the problem is, discern the appropriate source of help. Draw on your inner wisdom and outside resources. Make use of every contact you have to identify all possible sources. Identify questions that allow you to check out those different sources, and weigh whether or not they are qualified to assist you.

Unfortunately, when I was losing my job and caught up in both spiritual and mental turmoil, I never did this kind of thoughtful analysis. I just ran from helper to helper, asking people to tell me what to do, never fully describing the nature of the crisis.

I was failing at work and I was getting nightmares and flashbacks of my early childhood trauma. The person I most trusted to advise me was not from my immediate and most trusted community but was an acquaintance whom I called because she was the only person I knew who had been in a mental hospital, and I knew I was close to needing that. I was making choices out of fear, not out of my inner wisdom. She was the one who advised me to go on retreat. She never stopped and said, "Why are you calling me, Annie? Aren't there people who know you better?"

If I had asked myself the question, "What is my problem?" I never would have gone on retreat, because I would have realized that one of my problems was psychological not spiritual. And had I not dismissed the other problem—failing at work—I might have realized that I also needed help dealing with my career, help in deciding how to resolve my job failure and where to go next. Instead, I simply abandoned my career out of distress and refused the outplacement benefits that my company offered me when I was fired.

But let me give you an example as well of what *did* work.

When I was back on my feet after the fourth psychotic episode, I knew by then that my problem was psychological and that the help I most needed was a skilled and heartfelt therapist. I had actually known that earlier and pursued looking for someone, but the woman I chose, after talking with my psychiatrist, refused to see me. So that door closed. Her refusal taught me to wait, and it taught me to trust that the door had closed because I was not ready.

So a few months later, when my psyche opened to my childhood trauma, I knew that, yes, this was when to look for a new therapist. The signal came not from the "let's-get-this-show-on-the-road" part of me—the unhealthy "ego"—but from my inner world.

I began asking people who I trusted whom they would suggest as a therapist. I asked my psychiatrist, a 12-Step program friend, and a professional on the staff of the trauma unit at the nearby psychiatric hospital. I then checked out each of the people they suggested. I had my own list of questions to identify whether they were skilled and heartfelt.

That process worked well for me. It resulted in my finding a therapist whom I trust more than anyone else I've ever worked with. And I knew it as soon as I heard her voice. My intuitive knowing is much more developed now. It's not crowded out by the fear and desperation I felt in years past. I have a well-contained life, having worked to build that container since I left the hospital. That container meant I wasn't desperate. I could operate within God's timeframe, not my own.

What makes "help" work? How does a climate of trust get built? How does an experiencer know whom to trust and how does a helper create a climate where the experiencer can level with others?

I didn't learn any of this in a systematic fashion. I just stumbled through, but maybe after years of stumbling I can pass on to you a bit of what I've learned.

First, be discerning about whom you trust. Be careful about who tell your experiences to. In other words, don't trust everyone. Both mystical experiences and mental illness fill lots of people with fear, which means they won't be able to help. And, of course, the best help comes from people who have been where you are—not always, but sometimes. And most people have not had those kinds of experiences.

Second, know that it's OK if is is difficult to be totally honest about what you are experiencing. You have good reasons for that. Both *mysticism* and *mental illness* are surrounded with stereotypes that make leveling difficult.

Third, start slowly. Begin testing the trust level by sharing a little bit of your experience. Then see how the potential helper responds. If the response is helpful, go on. If not—and you may want to try a couple of times—then say goodbye and look for another helper.

Fourth, look for love. Personal chemistry is as important as skill.

Fifth, don't assume that all professionals know what they are doing, because they don't. I consciously put myself in the hands of some professionals who did not know what they were doing, simply because they were the best I could find. And, at times, you have to compromise, knowing that this person is only temporary. However, don't be too quick to settle for someone, just because they have the right credentials.

Sixth, don't hesitate to ask questions of potential helpers. Find out if they have had experiences like yours or are experienced in helping people like you. You have the right to ask whatever questions you want. All helpers can do is refuse to answer, and that's not the end of the world.

Seventh, realize that you may benefit from different kinds of helpers at different times in your journey. I was able to trust different kinds of people at different times, depending on how severe my crisis was, what other sources of support I had, and how much fear I was up against. The more fearful I was, the harder it was to trust anyone, and the more I needed someone who was deeply anchored in the spiritual world.

During one of my most fearful times, when I could trust no one else, I trusted a friend who was deeply centered in God. The kicker is that in some ways, especially psychologically, she was not trustworthy. She had difficulty setting boundaries with me; she had no psychological training; and she had a life already stretched thin between family and work. Yet for years, of all the people in my life, she was the one person that I really trusted. She was willing to love. I could tell her pieces of my experience that I could not tell anyone else. Even though she was not able to give me the skilled help that I needed, she was the best I could avail myself of, and I sure am glad I had her.

With many of the other people I went to for help, I was not able to share openly and honestly. I feel badly about that, because in most cases, they were skilled. Had I stuck it out with them, they probably would have been of more help to me than they were. Nothing replaces a weekly in-person therapy session when that is what is needed.

I did stick it out with one woman. I asked a woman whom I respected from 12-Step meetings to be my sponsor after my first psychotic episode. I asked her because I knew she could set boundaries and because she had strength and honesty. It seems odd to me now that I knew to ask her, because I didn't trust her emotionally. However, I had another friend that I completely trusted emotionally. And my sponsor's additional support was invaluable. Over a four-year period, she was far more help to me than any professional.

Different boundaries are helpful at different times. My differing relationships with these two friends illustrate the difference between how boundaries are handled in a spiritual context versus a psychological context. With the spiritual friend, I stepped into a spiritual reality that allowed us to connect deeply without the usual process of building trust, which takes time in a well-bounded relationship. The trust was simply given. The up side was that in a crisis I found someone who could carry me, and her carrying preserved me. The down side was that we never built an embodied relationship where the physical contexts of our lives were known to each other. She knew none of my history and so was operating just out of intuition. And because of that, she made some mistakes.

With my sponsor it was different. I had an embodied relationship. That's who she is: a landscape artist who immerses herself in the physical world. She is deeply spiritual, but in a very practical way. I saw her regularly at 12-Step meetings, and we talked on the phone once or twice a week. I never broke any boundaries with my sponsor. I always asked her if it was an OK time to talk, and sometimes it was not. With her I had a clear contract for support, with boundaries and clarity about the scope and limits of that contract. It took me years to be able to be open and honest with my sponsor. And to this day, she doesn't nurture me. But she does give me good guidance.

As I mature in these two relationships, they grow more alike. I now have good boundaries with both, and I take in warm support from my sponsor. Over the years, I have needed both of them.

What makes help good? Help is good when it is not controlling, when it is willing to "be with" as much as direct, when it can be both warm and confrontive, when it is flexible, when it is heartfelt, when it is willing to take charge when necessary, when it loves, when it knows its own limitations.

A good helper will encourage the experiencer to identify her inner wisdom and to act from that. A good helper will suggest that the experiencer put herself in places where she feels safe and can access her inner wisdom. And the good helper will support the experiencer in acting on that wisdom.

Quakers, by and large, are good at doing this kind of thing. However, this has a dangerous side as well; at least it did for me. For much of my crisis, I could not access my inner wisdom. It was blocked by fear and shame. So helpers who encouraged me to act on what I thought was a "leading" were not helpful. My sense of what was right for me was off. I have gotten more help from people experienced in dealing with abuse survivors. They know the patterns that I struggle with, and they can confront those patterns.

If a helper's sense of leading conflicts with the experiencer's, I think they need to level with each other about that. It is sometimes hard for a helper and an experiencer to really team with each other, rather than one deferring to the other. When they have different leadings, maybe it would be wise to seek out a third person who could discern the "right" way to go. In short, what helpers most need to do is to love, to listen, and to confront.

In our living and growing, we can become open to that which has previously been unconscious, but we must recognize that there comes a point when we need to stop opening ourselves and deal with what we have. In valuing growth, Annie may have opened herself to too much and too fast before she had a way of containing her openings.

All of us are different. Annie believes it would have been easier for her to build her container in familiar surroundings. Others have sometimes found that they need new surroundings to integrate their experiences. A good match between the container and what is to be contained is important.

Some in the psychiatric profession can be very helpful when intense abuse and trauma issues arise. Recently, when I asked Annie if she is well, she responded, "I am doing well because now I know what is well and what is ill and where to get the help I need to deal with what is ill. It was very helpful to tell my story to someone who truly wanted to hear it and could find the gifts in it when I could not. And it is equally helpful to find people who can help me solve problems."

Annie has been such a blessing. Her journey has been incredibly courageous, and she has taught me so much about this process of finding the right kind of help. She is now employed, has many great friends, has a faith community, and has many other groups she is a part of. She reports being happy much of the time. She is no longer so fearful about the possibility of further breakdowns.

Sometimes I feel like her cheerleader. I find myself wanting to yell at the top of my lungs, "Go, Annie!" Cheerleading is a needed role in spiritual friendship. Congratulating one another and celebrating our successes are really important.

In the next chapter, we'll look more specifically at listening and talking with those who have had extraordinary experiences, for in many cases, effective listening and talking are among the most important ways of creating the kind of community in which congratulations and celebration—and even outright cheerleading—are natural outcomes.

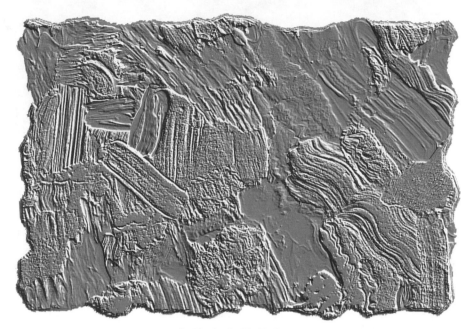

CHAPTER 10

*"God's presence is
not destroyed by
our mistakes or by
our experiences that
appear crazy . . ."*

Creating Community:
Listening and Talking

L ISTENING TO PEOPLE talk about
their extraordinary experiences is not
always easy.

Most of us have had varying degrees of augmented experience:
special moments when our child was born or when a loved one died,
perhaps a feeling evoked by art or poetry. Sometimes, when we tell
others about our experience, it helps rekindle a similar special awareness in them. In such cases, the experience of the listener is a treasure
and a joy. However, if the story is something quite far from our experience, we can be frightened by its content.

Suspending belief or disbelief is important in listening. But sometimes we do not let go of our fear of the foreign-ness of the other's reality, and we feel the need to protect ourselves. The presentation of da-
ta that does not match our own perceptions of reality can be disturb-
ing.

Sometimes we get disturbed because it is time for us to broaden
our horizons and open into a bigger reality, and that can be threaten-

ing. But sometimes the other reality is just not a place we want to go.

Earlier, I shared some of Paula's story, and I want to share a bit more of it here as a prelude to a further exploration of talking and listening.

BASKING IN THE PRESENCE VS. FEELING THE 'CREEPS'
Paula's experience of listening to others' extraordinary journeys

When I hear others describe their mystical experiences, I have a variety of responses.

With some, I have an almost intuitively positive response. My breathing slows. I relax. I know I am in the presence of someone who has shared the kind of experience I have had. I take great pleasure in hearing their stories and basking in this sense of sharing the Presence.

But there are two kinds of reports that I experience negatively, and sometimes they appear in combination.

I find myself wary when someone is trying to sell me on an intellectual scheme for understanding both his or her experience and mine. I don't mind hearing how someone else explains his or her own experience. But I am wary of those who want me to think of my own experience in the same way.

The other wariness comes when the experience is just too far out for me to wrap my mind around. Now, let me say that my mind has been stretched over the past several years, so less and less falls in this category. But I did wonder a bit about the woman who believes herself to be channeling a computer program that is going to revolutionize something or other on this earth. But, who knows, maybe she is, and maybe it will.

Then there was a man that I got to know fairly well whose mystical experiences were intertwined with both a deep craving to be loved and a penchant for telling about his sexual experiences. I feel confident that he *did* have what I would regard as genuine mystical experiences, but I was uneasy hearing about the rest. He gave me the creeps.

I guess that's another test: the creeps. Let me see if I can describe the creeps, as I call it. It includes anxiety in the pit of my stomach and a feeling of confusion. I begin to wonder if I really have to take this in. Even now, as I think about some of what I've heard, I find myself making faces. I guess when I have anxiety in the pit of my stomach, feel confused, and want to make faces, I have the creeps.

Some of Paula's observations seem almost universal. For example, it's easier to listen to someone whose experiences seem similar to our own than someone whose experiences seem very different. And when we do encounter those whose experiences go beyond what we have previously understood, it's always easier when they don't try to make us feel like we have to take on their understanding of such experiences for ourselves. Likewise, few of us want to have someone else impose their own intellectual schemes or interpretations on our own experience.

Paula's description of what she calls "the creeps" is a great way of knowing when one's boundaries feel invaded. For each of us, those boundaries might fall in a slightly different place. Cultural norms can make a difference as well. But when those boundaries are invaded, it is awfully difficult to be a good listener.

Paula uses an example of a man who had a penchant for sharing descriptions of his personal, sexual experiences. A boundary had been crossed, and he gave her "the creeps." She needed to protect herself. Another common violation of boundaries involves the intellect. Paula mentions that she doesn't mind hearing how other people explain things to themselves, but she is wary of efforts to impose their own thinking on her. For most of us, whenever someone tells us what we ought to think or believe, that is a violation of our intellectual boundaries, our desire to form our own ideas about things.

Because each of us has different boundaries on these issues, it's important to be clear with ourselves about where those boundaries lie—and to communicate those boundaries to others—so that together we can see that they are respected.

Broken boundaries aren't the only problem. Other things can also get in the way of creating the kind of community where respectful talking, genuine listening, and helpful celebrating can occur. We need to learn constructive ways of using our rage and our terror so that we can be our authentic selves with God and others.

I remember a life-transforming experience many years ago when I was having a really difficult time. I had finished graduate school and was excited about teaching, but some things were just not right for me in the academic environment. One day—after checking to make sure that my neighbors were not home—I just started screaming at God. I was so angry I could hardly see straight. No, I *actually* couldn't see straight. I was convinced that God had really screwed up and I was mad. I screamed and wailed and cried and whined and cussed and more.

Suddenly a calm came over me like I had never felt, and I got an image of God smiling and saying, "It's about time you got more real. It's OK. I can handle any amount of fear or rage you can generate."

It was incredibly liberating. I am very careful about whether there are other people around, but I now have no qualms about saying, "God, I love you, and I am really mad at you about this." I have found that being totally honest about my feelings is healthy. It helps me keep my rage and my fear felt and not suppressed.

This kind of primal release is also important as we try to create a community in which significant talking and listening can occur—talking and listening not just about mundane matters but talking and listening that fosters the creation of critical containers for experiences that go beyond the ordinary.

SAFETY OF A CLUSTER
Suzanne's story of using groups to frame her journey

As I understand it, the mystical encompasses out-of-body experiences, reincarnation, and visions. I teach literature, and many people in my literary work are mystical.

My own mystical experiences have accompanied primal therapy. They have not involved seeing God or Christ. It has been more a state of awareness or a sense of being.

Often that which is spiritual is labeled crazy.

In my family, for example, there is much depression and mental illness. My sister goes to a therapist and takes drugs. I do primal therapy and no drugs. But my family gets worried because my therapy is so intense. But after primal, I feel good spiritually. I feel an expansiveness—it's good!

During primal, I have mystical experiences. I just get into a padded box and do crazy things. What I do, I *need* to do. I get in touch with God-self and that is linked with my spiritual journey.

I lived for a time in a community that did not harm anything— even fleas. They communicate and tell them they don't want them. They are living beautifully what they believe. They don't harm roaches, rats, or anything. It's hard for awhile; then it works. Generosity of spirit is important. It is an alternative community, and the people there are often called "weirdos" as they don't work 9-to-5 jobs but instead focus on intentional community. I learned about primal therapy because they often do it to deal with stress.

There is resistance for me in this because my family doesn't believe in it. Most therapists don't want to do long-term therapy, and I have felt much pressure to go on medications.

My friends and I see our practice as spiritual, even though there is no facility within the tradition for it. I live with my God-self—and keep living.

Nervous breakdowns are seriously underrated in this society as a process of spiritual transformation, a spiritual awakening. It's often said that if we have nervous breakdowns, we are alienated. But from the perspective of those on the outside, lots of people who choose a spiritual life have "wacko" experiences. Yet in the safety of a cluster, they are seen as spiritual experiences. Look at all the things that happen in a church. Breakdown is a luxury, an opportunity for something new to emerge.

In my experience, community support has allowed me to be who I am—and to do what I need to do without stigma.

Suzanne's story points to another aspect of building containers. People need groups, communities in which to frame their experiences. People having intense experiences of God need to share them with others in a place where spirits can connect with one another. Faith communities have served this purpose for centuries.

Unfortunately, as the following story illustrates, not everyone finds the support they need when they turn to their faith community.

LONGING TO BE ACCOMPANIED
Liza's story of longing for spiritual support

I am in the process of leaving my meeting. It is very painful because I have been a member for many years. But for the last year, I have been on a very lonely spiritual quest. The meeting was very supportive when I went through a divorce and had to make many life changes. But they cannot meet me when I need company in this deep spiritual place. I am sad about that.

It is a good meeting. They do much good work. They are very supportive when people have problems. They are good social workers. But my need now is for something different. There is an important piece missing in my meeting.

Recently on a retreat we were asked to reflect on a deep spiritual moment in a worship-sharing context. Everyone spoke about how great the meeting was when members have problems. But no one spoke about a deeply spiritual experience.

I don't think the meeting wants to—or even can—go beyond being nice. So I have a deep sense of an important piece being missing.

> Fellowship is important. Social work is important. But being accompanied to that deep place of the Spirit is the heart of what we are about as a faith community, and I long for that.

Liza's message resonates. It functions as a concise description of what many have said. Our containers may provide fellowship. They may address problems and even provide support to help people solve those problems. But a great need for many people is a faith community where they can share their deepest spiritual experiences—and be accompanied with Love in that journey.

It's important here to acknowledge a distinction between social work and psychology on the one hand and accompaniment on the other. The social worker is in problem-solving mode. Experiences are framed as problems to be solved or something to be fixed or changed. But for those having experiences of God, the need is not for problem-solving. The need is for loving accompaniment.

Our role in accompaniment usually involves deep listening and sharing. Eldering, which involves accountability and support, may also be needed in a loving way. Usually, however, accompaniment is distinct from problem-solving.

In listening to many participant's stories, I have distilled several points of wisdom on the process of containment and accompaniment. I share these points here with many thanks to those who have shared them with me:

❖ Different kinds of help are helpful at different times.
❖ Those whose journeys include out-of-the-ordinary experiences must be willing to seek and receive help.
❖ There is a difference between helping and rescuing.
❖ Providing someone with the information and resources that they need is usually helpful.
❖ In a crisis, the presence of other humans is crucial.
❖ Those with out-of-the-ordinary experiences often need help discerning the nature of their experience.
❖ Those who are having such experiences then need to discern for themselves what help they need.
❖ Experiencers must carefully discern whom to talk to, knowing that the words *mysticism* and *mental illness* sometimes evoke fear in others.
❖ When a listener is chosen, those with experiences to share should start slowly and see how it goes. If

the conversation proves helpful, go on. If it's un-helpful, say good-bye and find another listener.

❖ Have a list of questions to ask any professionals that you are considering using, and pay attention to how they answer your questions.

❖ Look for love.

❖ Different kinds of helpers with different kinds of boundaries are helpful at different times.

❖ Remember that the more fearful the one is who has had out-of-the-ordinary experiences, the harder it will be to trust the helper.

❖ Good help is not controlling. It usually comes from a helper who is willing to support the experiencer in moving through "that deep place of the Spirit."

❖ Good help is both warm and confrontive. It's flexible, heartfelt, and loving.

❖ The best help normally comes from helpers who know their limits.

Everything that I have learned in this project related to discernment on the spiritual journey can be summed up in a Taoist story about a farmer whose horse ran away.

That first evening, his neighbors gathered to commiserate with him since this was such bad luck. The farmer said, "May be."

The next day the horse returned, but it brought with it six wild horses, and the neighbors came exclaiming at his good fortune. He said, "May be."

And then, the following day, the farmer's son tried to ride one of the wild horses. He was thrown and broke his leg. Again the neighbors came to offer their sympathy for the misfortune. The farmer said, "May be."

The day after that, conscription officers came to the village to seize young men for the army, but because of the broken leg the farmer's son was rejected. When the neighbors came in to say how fortunately everything had turned out, he said, "May be."

Likewise, in our spiritual journeys, we are constantly trying to sort through the possibilities and choose our direction. I have come to believe that we are simply to do our best. That is all that God requires. We are simply to have faith. We will make mistakes along the way, but as we are met by God, our mistakes will be transformed into good. Romans 8:28 says, "All things work together for good to them that love God, to them who are called according to his purpose" (KJV).

In doing our best, we are to utilize our gifts to make choices in the best way we know how in the moment. Our movement toward freer choice is a journey of letting go of limitations. It is a journey toward healing and freedom.

When I began this writing project, I was confronted with language around discernment that did not fit with my own experience or with that of many with whom I have talked. I began the project hearing questions about "authentic" versus "inauthentic" or "true" versus "delusional" experiences of God. I have not found that language useful. Experiences just happen. They just are. When we determine that an experience of God is delusional or false, it promotes greater dissociation of the parts of ourselves—and that can weaken us.

When someone describes a vision, a voice, or another encounter with the Divine, questions like "is this real?" are not usually a productive line of questioning for discernment. Our shared perception of "reality" is just that: a shared perception. As long as we share our reality with others and they share with us, we remain in a part of a shared reality with others. That is a usual definition of sanity in this culture.

It seems to me that the distinctions we make between the psychological and the spiritual and between the physical and the spiritual are arbitrary distinctions that humans have used to develop human institutions. God did not make us as psychological and physical and spiritual creatures. God just made us. The distinctions that we make are for the purpose of enriching our lives. When they do not serve that purpose, we need to remember that our parts need not be separated in such ways. God understands both psychology and neurochemistry.

God's presence is not destroyed by our mistakes or by experiences that appear crazy. All experiences hold the capacity for serving God's purposes. Our experiences cannot be judged by their content but can be examined to see how they fit into our mystical spiritual journeys. We are required to carefully examine our lives to do the best we know in the moment. And we are asked to have faith that God will meet us and use our lives even if we mess up.

In the literature, one can find many reports of psychological analyses of pathology in the lives of many spiritual leaders. Some may find it amusing to read psychological evaluations done on Jesus, Saint Paul, or George Fox, but whose life is enriched by such reports?

My own leading is in quite the opposite direction. We can acknowledge and address problems that arise in living, but rather than searching out the pathology, I would like to see us building the containers that help us in finding the gifts and using them to enrich our lives and the lives of the communities of which we are a part.

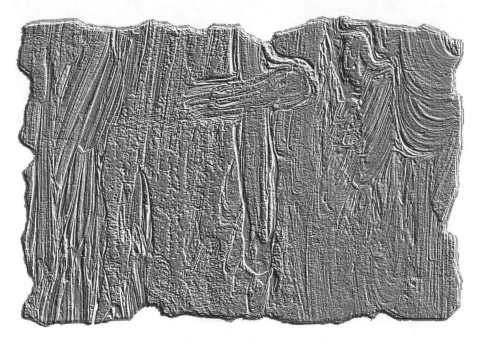

CHAPTER 11

"What many people
need most is a place
to share their
experiences without
preconditions . . ."

Golden Nuggets:
Lessons and Concerns

FOR ME AS the researcher, being involved in this project has been like being placed in a very rich gold mine. The gold is sometimes covered with soil or leaves or other natural elements. But with a bit of digging and polishing, the gold nuggets shine.

One shining treasure is the stark diversity of the experiences that have been shared. I find each one precious. And each one has been filled with treasured insights.

Another shining treasure has come in the widely varied reports about psychiatric helping relationships: from horrendous to terrifically helpful. In the differences, there is much to learn.

Finally, I have found many rich "nuggets" in the traditional Quaker practice of containment, integration, and discernment. I myself am a Quaker, and this project was undertaken in a largely Quaker context. So it's not surprising that I find value in the reports of these Quaker responses. However, my strong hunch is that many beyond the Quaker world will find value in them as well.

So before I move on to consider some important points for both mental health professionals and religious communities, I would like to examine some of the golden nuggets that have been uncovered, some of the valuable insights that seemed to recur again and again in the stories that were told.

As I listened to these stories, I was reminded again and again that when we are opened to the presence of God, WE BRING ALONG THE FULL RANGE OF OUR HUMANNESS. This may include our fear, our anger, even our less-than-fully-developed self. Do these psychological issues invalidate our experiences of God? I think not.

Stories heard in the course of this project convinced me that the mystical experience can even be superimposed on a wide spectrum of experiences that are often framed as affecting one's mental health. Several participants, for example, had experienced trauma in their childhood. Ironically, this trauma served to significantly open them, allowing God to speak. As a result, they brought the residue of their trauma into their adult lives—and into the Presence.

Their experiences demonstrate that not only can these kinds of things be worked through but they can actually be turned into good.

As I listened to these stories, I also heard MANY DIFFERENT DEFINITIONS of mysticism.

A wide range of experiences were labeled as mystical. Some of these experiences were calm, beautiful, and well-contained. Some involved intense energy. At times, fears and angers or other experiences made containing this energy difficult.

For some persons, the intensity of these experiences was so great and the resources on which they could draw so inadequate that they literally could not function. Some were hospitalized, and in some cases, the result was a diagnosis of some kind of mental illness.

Yet I've learned that while mystical experiences can differ greatly and can affect people in many different ways, there is a value and a divine gift to them all.

ACKNOWLEDGING AND VALUING SPIRITUAL DIVERSITY is the first step to achieving the kind of acceptance that has been a recurring theme in this project. It's the crux of what many are seeking.

When I began my study, I heard many supposedly knowledgeable Quakers expressing the belief that there is "a fine line" between mysticism and mental illness. But in talking with real people, sharing their real-life experiences, I found no evidence for that view, and the experiences that I heard fell along a broad continuum.

So in examining the relationship between mysticism and mental illness, I began with an either/or conceptualization and ended up with a both/and conceptualization—the "overlapping circles" model that I described in an earlier chapter.

Deeply spiritual experiences can and do cause an intensity to be created within a person. And often, when that energy comes into the body, one hears voices. One sees visions. Or perhaps one feels a Presence. This intensity typically interacts with other variables, especially the availability of nonpathological frameworks for understanding our experiences, and effective support from others who do not fear our experiences. What I found was that these are among the most important factors in influencing whether a person's intense experiences are eventually integrated in a positive way.

In Quaker circles, I have often heard people say that you can know an experience is of God if it brings peace. But OVERLY SPECIFIC CRITERIA CAN MISDIRECT THE DISCERNMENT PROCESS. Such criteria, for example, can cause people to be uncomfortable in sharing their "unpeaceful" experiences.

Growth—as well as peace—are signs that we have been touched by God. And growth does not come peacefully to all of us. As we grow with God, some of us may find ourselves kicking and screaming. Eventually, the growth may indeed bring peace, but it's not always peaceful at first.

In like manner, just because psychological issues accompany an experience of God, that doesn't mean that the experience is invalid or delusional. When we impose too rigid a standard for discerning the validity of an experience of God, we build walls. Yet what many people need most is a place to share their experiences without preconditions and a place where they can do so in a spirit of wholeness.

It says something to me that so many people—with so little prompting—came forth to participate in this research. It says that more people than we readily acknowledge are having out-of-the-ordinary experiences of God.

A great variety of experiences of God appear within the realm of the out-of-the-ordinary. For example, many in our culture would consider hearing voices as pathological. Yet many people acknowledge hearing voices—and many different kinds of voices.

So what we need to remember is that GOD IS BIG. Thus the manifestations of God are many. The Spirit is gifting many people in many different ways—ways that we need to acknowledge and be grateful for.

As a result of this project, I have come to realize that the experiences that our culture tends to see as out-of-the-ordinary—voices, visions, presences—are actually far more common than I imagined. And the continuums along which these experiences fall are so varied that there are simply no easy or conclusive ways of automatically separating "mysticism" from "mental illness." Criteria that seem to work in some cases end up not working in others.

Many of us recognize that **"US" VERSUS "THEM" DUALITIES CAN BE HARMFUL,** especially when the division—as is so often the case—functions to ensure the power of the "us" over the "them." Such separations can perpetuate the notion, for example, that rich is in and poor is out, that white is good and black is bad, or that male is strong and female is weak.

When dualities are set up, certain people start thinking of themselves as better that those who they perceive to be their "opposite." Great harm can be done thereby to those who are thus disempowered.

The stories told by participants make clear that equally destructive are the dualities that are often set up between "crazy" and "not crazy," "abnormal" and "normal," "delusional experience" and "true experience." When people have experiences of God, they are just having experiences. There is no need to categorize. Setting up a duality is not necessary.

We need to accept that significant experiences happen to all of us. Some of these significant experiences involve mystical encounters with God.

Integrating these experience into our lives takes much energy, and I believe that that's what we need to focus on—instead of spending our time sorting things into the kinds of categories that can so easily lead to yet another disempowering duality. After all, isn't mysticism itself in part a transcending of dualities?

As I listened to story after story from those who shared this project with me, I also came to feel that the **RELATIONSHIP BETWEEN LOVE AND FEAR** is intimately connected in some way to the relationship between mysticism and mental illness.

In her book *A Return to Love,* Marianne Williamson has written:

> Love is what we are born with. Fear is what we learn. The
> spiritual journey is the unlearning of fear and prejudices and the
> acceptance of love back into our hearts. Love is the essential

reality and our purpose on earth. To be consciously aware of it, to experience love in ourselves and others, is the meaning of life. Meaning does not lie in things. Meaning lies in us.

Many participants described a dance that goes back and forth between fear and love, a dance that they feel caught up in.

Consider, for example, this simple letter that one participant wrote to God:

> Dear God,
>
> What is the proper relationship between love and fear that leads to serving you?

I was told that the reply that came was this:

> Dear Child of Mine,
>
> One must send divine Love to fear. One must treat fear with respect. Love is kind, and Love is gentle. And Love is Love. Love does not give itself over to fear. Love shares its abundant self with fear but does not become fear. I am with you in all of it.

In the Friends meeting I attend, a young man ministered to us, saying, "That which we resist, persists." In another ministry, a young woman recited a quote from an unknown source that says, "Love is the only rational response." It seems that a loving response in the presence of fear is not only the "right" response but is also the only effective response.

We all have prejudices. We all have people we react to negatively before we even get to know them. When we can remove the glasses through which we automatically see, in order to see more clearly what is there, we are often surprised by the goodness that we might have missed if we had not rationally and intentionally chosen to respond with love. Fear is persistent, but when invited to tea and when its gifts are examined, I find it ready to move on rather quickly, for it is quite fragile in the face of Divine Love.

Although many of the participants in this study spoke freely of being torn between love and fear, the truth is that we all perform this dance every day.

Participants have taught me that instead of condemning those who acknowledge their fears, we need to create places in our lives—and in the lives of those around us—in which moving toward the Love will become not only more possible but more natural.

The more I listened to people's stories, the more a concern arose in my heart. I realized that many people in our world are not talking about their experiences because they believe it is unsafe to do so.

I heard repeatedly from participants that these experiences of God were among the most important experiences in their lives. A good many told me that they had talked about their experiences with no one—or maybe with only one or two others—even when they needed help to understand and contain their experiences.

During the very first story that I heard, the participant confided that she had shared her story with almost no one. By the third story, the participant confided that she had never before talked about this experience. I did not expect that, yet I heard it over and over.

Why can't these contemporary individuals talk about their most important, most life-transforming experiences? The risk is too great. They are afraid that their most precious experiences will be dismissed or ridiculed and that they themselves will be labeled as crazy, abnormal, or delusional. That is just too painful to risk.

I have thought about this situation, wondering what has influenced us and our culture to create such an unfortunate situation. I can't claim to have come up with a comprehensive list of such influences, but four things do come to mind: 1) theological perspectives, 2) traditional psychiatric practice, 3) the cultural unacceptability of fear and anger, and 4) historical precedents.

I'd like to look at each of these influences in greater detail.

THEOLOGICAL PERSPECTIVES are the first factor that I think contributes to people not sharing their experiences of God. Part of the theology that underlies many current religious beliefs is the notion that God "spoke" to people in the days of the Bible—and that early Christians may have heard the "voice of God"—but that God simply does not do things that way now.

A man that I will call Bobby came to see me. He had heard that I was doing this project. He was unable to tell me much of his story, but he did say that at age twenty-one he heard a voice that he believed to be God telling him that he was to be a monk. When he shared this with his priest, the priest told him that God does not speak to people through "voices." Bobby became very confused. In talking with me, he described his life as having become "chaotic." Medical professionals had told him that he is schizophrenic.

I could not help but wonder how Bobby's life may have been different if the voice he heard had been taken seriously. If the priest had encouraged him to explore the voice's message in a positive way, would his life have turned chaotic? Would he have not been labeled schizophrenic?

TRADITIONAL PSYCHIATRIC PRACTICE has been to label experiences of God—as opposed to beliefs about God—as delusional. The content of such experiences has often been suppressed through therapy or medication or whatever it takes. For decades, people were not listened to and were medicated to suppress uncomfortable content.

As I will discuss in a later chapter, at least in some circles, things are changing. But change is slow, and a psychiatric legacy of judgment and suppression has discouraged people from sharing with others precious experiences that might be misunderstood.

Tragically, THE CULTURAL UNACCEPTABILITY OF FEAR AND ANGER not only remains strong but often serves to make the sharing of stories difficult.

Our culture seems to assume that only when we are "together" can good things happen, and being "together" is typically defined as being free of any anger or fear or any other kind of inner turmoil. Anything connected with what is sometimes called a "dark night journey"—a lonely time during which one's direction and calling is unclear—is often viewed as something to be avoided.

Even in the religious world, fear and anger, because of their potential for destruction, have been deemed to be "not of God." The potential gifts of such turmoil is seldom acknowledged. And this has led to the silencing of mystics who have otherwise desired to share their experiences.

The dark night journey first described by St. John of the Cross and more recently explored by Sandra Cronk is an integral part of the mystical experience, but it is often suppressed, even by Friends.

In a recent ministry, Doreen Hardy said:

> I have an image of Jesus on the cross calling, 'My God, my God, why hast thou forsaken me?' I always thought that was a moment of weakness on his part. Today, I see such a moment as a necessary part of Jesus' life, just as it is in ours. It is that moment that gives us the capability for divine compassion for others and for the world, should we choose the path of faith.

Unfortunately, this potential for good is often overlooked, even in the religious community. All of this contributes to a cultural negativity toward inner fears and turmoils that makes it difficult for many with mystical experiences to share the full range of their transforming experiences.

In collecting my stories, I heard many people say that they experienced a bleak and lonely period in their lives and that their current ministry —whether on a personal or social level—emerged from that loneliness. While I was a Gest fellow at Haverford College, I read the stories of many Quaker writers and ministers who said the same thing. Despite the fact that they hadn't *chosen* these experiences—and would, in fact, not *choose* to go through them again—these dark nights led to the mornings during which life opened up for them in new and holy ways.

Night journeys are an important tool in God's work. They can change our lives. They can increase our faith. Sandra Cronk calls them a "re-patterning" of our lives. What a shame that, due to cultural and religious prejudices, many feel denied an opportunity to share with others the ways in which God has worked in their lives for good.

HISTORICAL PRECEDENTS also play a role.

Many religious groups have experienced persecution, injustice, and misunderstanding. Quakerism is one of those groups. And whether we are a part of a group that was judged and ridiculed for its religious experiences, the mere knowledge of such precedents can cause us to shy away from anything that might subject us to similar ridicule or injustice.

Quakerism, for example, was formed during a time when men and women were having intense experiences of God. This gave them energy for spreading what they saw as a new Truth. A societal backlash occurred, and many early Quakers were imprisoned or tortured when they spoke their Truths. The literature of those writing against early Quakers is vicious. As a result, many Quakers became quiet about their intense experiences of God. Although accounts of miracles performed by George Fox, an early leader of Quakerism, can be read by us today, they were deliberately omitted from early published versions of his journal. Fearing continued persecution, the editors felt that it was necessary to leave out some of Fox's most intense experiences of God. They wanted to "protect" Quakerism so that it would survive.

Such precedents may have seemed a good political strategy at the time, but regardless of which religious tradition we identify with, such strategies may have also had strongly negative spiritual consequences.

Social and cultural backlashes are always possible. But is it really wise for people to remain quiet about their experiences of God? Might it not be possible, as some of the Gospels suggest, that it is in risking our lives that we truly find them? And might it not be a tremendous gift to others if we were to risk talking about our experiences?

Many commentators have suggested that our society has moved so far in the direction of endless materialism that a deep spiritual hunger pervades. Others suggest that among the causes underlying the contemporary increase in mental illness, especially depression, are such things as fear, anger, underdeveloped selves—and, significantly, spiritual hunger.

I believe that this hunger is so strong in our culture today that many would be blessed by more people speaking more openly about their mystical experiences of God. In fact, since I began this project, literally hundreds of people have told me of their need for companionship and accompaniment through a dark night journey that has been a part of their own spiritual experience. Yet sometimes our knowledge of history incapacitates us.

I'm grateful for every golden nugget that was shared with me in the course of this study. I'm grateful for the lessons that participants' imparted. And I long for the day in which those theological, psychiatric, cultural, and historical factors which tend to block the freer sharing of such stories will be more widely overcome.

Meanwhile, on the pages that follow, I offer a brief interlude in the form some of the paintings that emerged from my hands in the course of this project. Many were created in response to the stories and the insights that were being shared with me.

Mystical experiences are multidimensional in character, and so it seems only appropriate for this book to be multidimensional as well.

INTERLUDE:
PAINTINGS

As I listened to people's stories of their experiences of God, many paintings came. They seemed to be gifts to me. In time, words from various stories came to be associated with the paintings.

I share these with you here in an attempt to convey some of the multidimensional character of our common journeys toward a deeper reality.

I hope that you will enter the creations on the next eight pages with a listening ear and an opened eye. What you see here came from that deep place of connection with the Spirit of creation energy, that "place from where the words come."

JENNIFER ELAM

The activity of the Spirit is like a volcano, with lava flowing just under the surface of the earth—then, on occasion, there is an eruption of Spirit energy

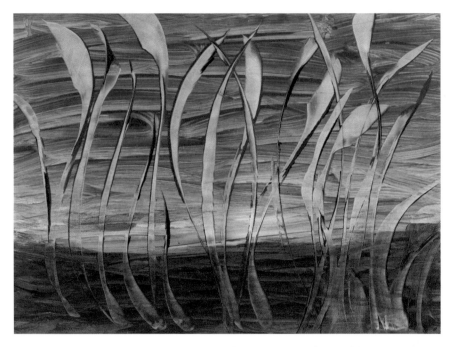

The conflict among Quakers is like a stormy sea:
the deeper you go, the calmer the water becomes

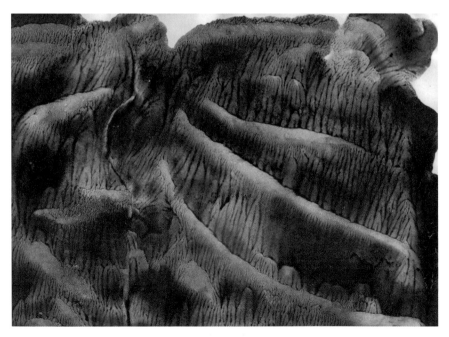

Listen in that deep place from where the words come

My Spirituality Blossoms

I saw the same gray-white homespun woolen robes next to me and felt the warmth of someone who had been walking in the sun

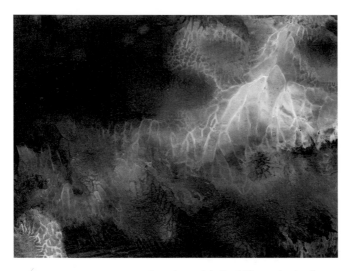

Dancing with God Through the Storm

The storm subsides:
from breakdown
to breakthrough

An image of fire

Pulled as if by gravity to that place where opposites meet

Hands ReBorn

The egg of my heart
births
my new hands

The egg cracks.
Searing, excruciating, clean pain
From my heart
emerges these hands

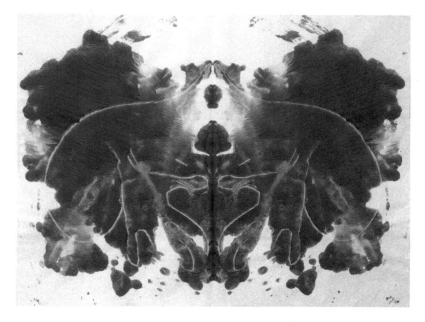

The hands falter, like a newborn colt

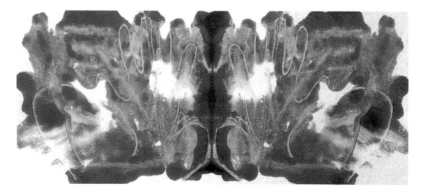

They turn in, I look at them in awe

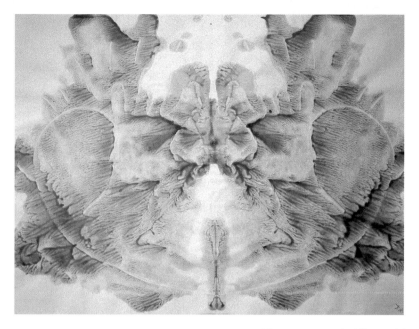

They turn out, holding gold

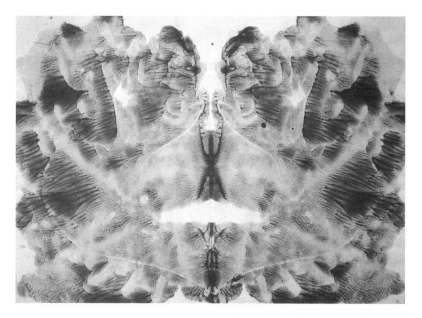

And move strongly into the world

The gold is distributed.

*Darkness responds and
is infused with Light*

*Light reaches toward the Darkness
to express love*

Kundalini awakening

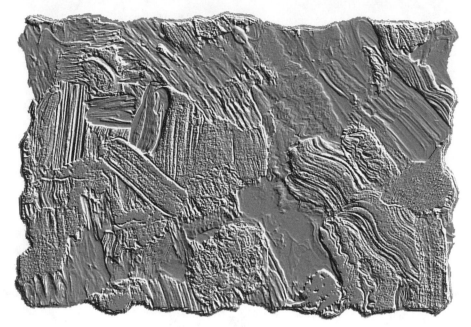

CHAPTER 12

*"A healthy, therapeutic
process, in which the
therapist understands
the spiritual journey,
can help us out of the
mire and into a
functioning life . . ."*

With Opened Eyes:
Roles for Therapy

*A*TRAIL OF ILL HEALTH *runs across
the story of the lives of many mystics,
and pathologists have always been
ready to discount the spiritual value of mysticism by showing it a near
neighbor to emotional diseases. . . . There [is] a school of theorists who tend
to "project" abnormality into everything. . . . We may want to take our place
among these "abnormals," as they have been the finest specimens of the
race . . .*

Rufus Jones in MYSTICAL RELIGION AND THE ABNORMAL

While many individuals have told me of their desire to "come out"
and talk about their experiences, a similar number have confessed
their deep fear of doing so. I understand that fear. I have felt that fear.
Sometimes I *still* feel that fear.

We are fearful because, to use the language of more than one participant in this study, "this is scary stuff." We are fearful because, to use
the language of Rufus Jones in his 1928 book, there is a school of the-

orists who tend to "project" abnormality onto anything and everything that they don't understand.

And perhaps we fear telling others of our most precious experiences because we know that there remains no more effective way of devaluing a person in this culture than by calling them "crazy" or "nuts." To have that label given to our most precious experiences can be devastating.

As a psychologist, I know that for decades my own profession did just that. In my basic training—and in the training of almost every psychologist that I have asked the question of—if one talked about experiences of God rather than just beliefs in God, it was considered delusional. As I mentioned earlier, that perspective has sometimes been validated by those theologians who somehow believe that while God talked to people in Bible days, there has been silence ever since.

I am happy to report, however, that I *have* found other professionals acknowledging that all mystical experiences are not the same. In fact, *The Diagnostic and Statistical Manual,* which is the primary guide used by the psychiatric profession for diagnosing mental disorders, was revised in 1994. A new category of "religious or spiritual problems" was added. These "religious or spiritual problems" were not listed as a disorder but as "conditions that can be the focus of clinical attention." That may be an important step forward.

Two years prior to this change, David Lukoff, a transpersonal psychologist at Saybrook Institute, had pointed to a "religiosity gap" between psychiatrists and their clients. And a few years before that, in a doctoral dissertation, psychologist Barbara Owen had cited some revealing statistics from the American Psychiatric Association and the American Psychological Association. While more than 90 percent of clients and the general public believe in God, only 5 percent of psychologists and 43 percent of psychiatrists profess such a belief. Past surveys have consistently shown that both the general public and psychiatric patients attend church more frequently, believe in God at a higher rate, and consider religion more important in their lives than do mental health professionals.

The change in *The Diagnostic and Statistical Manual* may encourage more careful assessments to be done in situations where clients bring their experiences of God to mental health professionals, rather than having such material automatically labeled as "delusion." Whether this will result in significant progress is not yet clear, but it *is* an important acknowledgement of the overlap between psychiatry and religion.

Since 1994, there has been a proliferation of professional literature on the assessment of religious or spiritual problems. Many "tests" of mystical and transcendent experiences have been proposed. One measure that is widely used is called the Mysticism Experiences Scale. It was developed by Ralph Hood in 1975. His definition of mystical experience includes the following criteria: loss of sense of self, unifying quality, perception of an inner subjectivity to all things, time and space modified, noetic quality, ineffability, positive affect, and a feeling of sacredness of the experience.

Lukoff has also developed measures of mysticism. His definition of mystical experience is "a transient, extraordinary experience marked by feelings of unity and harmonious relationship to the divine and everything in existence, as well as euphoric feelings, sense of gnosis, loss of ego functioning, alterations in time and space perception, and the sense of lacking control over the event." As you can see, current researchers tend to assess the "mystical experience" as an independent event, much as they might investigate the consciousness of a drug-induced experience.

I have tried to compare the classical mystical literature, including stories of the lives of ancient mystics, with the literature of those transpersonal psychologists who are studying contemporary mystical experiences. I see two major differences. First, transpersonal psychologists seldom address the importance of the *life* of the mystic. They focus on individual experiences rather than the fullness of one's life with God. Second, transpersonal psychologists tend to miss the importance of the lonely "dark night journey" that many mystics experience.

As I have mentioned earlier, Evelyn Underhill describes this "dark night" as an important stage of the mystical journey. It was first described in the sixteenth century by the mystic and contemplative, St. John of the Cross, who saw "the dark night" as a time of increasing faith. Sandra Cronk calls it one of the most powerful pathways in the journey to God, a time of stripping and emptiness. Although a person may feel that God is absent, although a person may feel caught up in meaninglessness, loss, and pain, it is often the time when God is doing the most powerful work in our lives, re-patterning our whole being.

This paradoxical path was mentioned by many participants in this study, individuals who have moved through such experiences on their way to ministry and wholeness. Yet even in the best literature of transpersonal psychology, written by professionals who are committed to finding ways of integrating psychology and spirituality, share perspectives, the "dark night" journey is often automatically relegated to the realm of the "abnormal" with its vast stigmatization and emphasis on pathology.

Don't take me wrong. Progress may have been made. Some researchers are now more carefully assessing consciousness. Some now recognize that certain non-rational states can have benefits. I applaud their work.

Ken Wilber, for example, is a writer who has developed a model that many transpersonal professionals find helpful. As I mentioned in an earlier chapter, he distinguishes pre-personal, personal, and transpersonal states of consciousness that occur along a spectrum. His is a hierarchical model in which mystical states are beneficial and are experienced by persons who have reached the personal and gone beyond. Problems can arise in using Wilber's model because in daily life, the pre-personal and the transpersonal often resemble one another: both non-rational.

Building from Wilber's model, psychiatrist Mitchell Liester has written about inner voices. Hearing the voice of God is a common experience. Liester is a psychiatrist in Colorado who has written on inner voices and believes they are not all pathological. He has developed a seven-point scale from pathological to transcendent. He believes that some voices are helpful. He calls these "transcendent voices. Others, he believes, are pathological, with many points in between. In a later work, Liester describes what he calls the "relativity theory of consciousness," suggesting a continuum similar to Wilber's but less hierarchical.

Liester's work hints at a question that I want to ask: can we look at all of the points along the continuum of consciousness as equal in value? Some therapists have, in fact, suggested this is possible. James Hillman, for example, recognizes the stigmatization that occurs in present conceptualizations of psychopathology and suggests a re-visioning, acknowledging the connection of "symptoms" to Jungian archetypes. Jungian analyst John Weir Perry goes a step further and describes the ways in which the "symptoms" of his patients diagnosed with schizophrenia can be positively used when their content is analyzed for archetypal meaning and clues about how their lives are to be transformed.

Similarly, Russell Lockhart discusses being trained in the older model in which the stories of people labeled with schizophrenia are seen as "crazy." Treatment involves punishment or at least ignoring the person. But he discovered that that way of being with people was unproductive. He writes:

> If the patient loses an opportunity to experience the meaning
> and purpose of his psychotic experience, he is victimized by a

"reality-oriented" therapeutic armamentarium that conspires against such realization. The therapist too must pay a price. He cannot allow himself to be enriched or even touched by the experience of the patient.

Haverford psychologist Judith Miller has built her practice on this idea. She seeks not to pathologize the "symptoms" of her clients diagnosed with schizophrenia but to normalize and use the experiences in positive ways. She seeks to help clients transform their lives by listening for the messages in their "symptoms." Although there are differences in the ability of people to function in our society, the focus of her efforts is on helping people to integrate the separated parts of their lives in positive ways to increase functioning. She has had good success.

My point in telling of the work of these professionals is to say that although traditional psychiatry has labeled voices, visions, presences, and other common experiences of God as delusional and has often suppressed them, there *are* professionals who seeing value in these experiences and are changing their practice accordingly.

Lukoff, for example, has described the stories of two people who had serious psychoses that were quite similar to one another. One was Allen Ginsberg; the other was a factory worker. After hospitalization, Ginsberg returned to a relatively accepting environment in New York where his psychoses were integrated into his poetry, and he became a great visionary artist. The factory worker returned to a sober, matter-of-fact life in a well-meaning but unimaginative community. His "potential visionary experience" became something that was "mere imagination."

Lukoff has suggested that "transpersonal professionals can play a role in improving the outcome from manic psychosis by broadening society's and the mental health system's acceptance of its potential for fostering personal growth." Since psychiatry has played a role in creating this situation in which we find ourselves, a situation in which people are afraid to talk about their experiences of God, I am encouraged that some professionals are trying to change that.

Mental health professionals have many tools for helping all of us improve our functioning in the world. They have good educational plans for solving problems, dealing with trauma, teaching skills for communication, and building relationships individually and in groups. They have important knowledge to share about how things tend to work in the physical world.

The use of professional tools can be very helpful—or quite problematic. Problems typically arise when the rules of behavioral science are applied too rigidly. Behavioral science provides us with valuable knowledge of tendencies in human behavior. But there are few *laws* of behavior. This may be because there is a spark of the divine in every human that makes overcoming all probabilities a possibility. Miracles that are beyond probabilities do happen.

Another problem is what has been referred to as the "religiosity gap." There are major differences in beliefs and practices related to God between mental health professionals and their clients. The client's beliefs and practices are more like the general lay public. The best mental health professionals strive to overcome any bias that they may feel about such experiences.

Professionals offer knowledge that can be very helpful. If clients can be aware of the tendency to focus on pathology—and choose for themselves what is pathological in their lives and what needs to be changed—professionals can serve them well. Tools for gaining a better awareness of the baggage that we all bring to adulthood can be very helpful in the kind of self-examination that is an important part of the spiritual journey. Commitment to a healthy, therapeutic process, in which the therapist understands the spiritual journey, can help us out of the mire and into a functioning life. It can help move us from being driven by our baggage toward clearer and freer choices about our lives.

Until our eyes are opened and we see our choices, we are too easily driven by our tendencies. Only with opened eyes can we transcend.

Years ago, Rufus Jones put it this way:

> One takes his dog to the art gallery in vain. . . . If nothing ever stirs a person's soul with hushed awe, if nothing ever makes him vibrant and palpitant because he feels himself in the presence of the in-breaking of the Divine, then there is no way to make that person comprehend what we mean by the essential aspect of religion. . . . *This* is defective and abnormal (italics added).

CHAPTER 13

"When we listen to
one another in
'that deep place
where words come
from,' we give each
other incredible
gifts . . ."

Religious Communities:
Releasing Transcendence

O UR CIVILIZATION *represses . . . any
form of transcendence. . . . Someone
with an insistent experience of other
dimensions, that he cannot entirely deny or forget, will run the risk of being destroyed by others, or of betraying what he knows. . . . Our "normal"
"adjusted" state is too often the abdication of ecstasy, the betrayal of our true
potentialities.*

R.D. Laing in The Divided Self

Twice before, I have shared with you portions of Helene's story.
Her story is a remarkable one in several respects, not the least of
which is that she and her mother Kate have felt wholly supported by
their Quaker meeting. Kate told me that the people in her meeting
have been there to help her with many issues as they have come up.
Helene, too, has felt warmly supported. She told me that it was most
helpful to know that the meeting was holding her in prayer.

Support from one's religious community can play a very positive role in any mystical journey. So I asked some of Helene's meeting members what it was that made it possible for them to support Helene and her family so well. I wondered if there was something here that other religious communities might benefit from.

They told me that it was easy to support people who are so easy to like. Individual personalities and one's facility for relationships undoubtedly play a role. They also said that Helene's personal openness was a big help, as well as the openness of her family in sharing what was happening and what their needs were. Knowing what one needs makes it much easier to get it for them. Clearly there are a multitude of variables related both to the religious community as a whole and to the one whose journey is taking mystical turns. Each makes a difference in a religious community's ability to function as an effective container.

Unfortunately, many people who are having intense mystical experiences have not yet found a religious community in which they feel safe talking about those experiences. "Containers" or "containment" were concepts that came up frequently in the stories I heard. Safe containers are places where people can share their experiences in ways that will make positive integration more likely. Religious communities of all kinds can help provide such containers, drawing on the best of their religious traditions.

Because I myself am a Quaker—and because most of my conversations with participants were held in Quaker contexts—it's easiest for me to show some of the ways in which basic Quaker testimonies can enlighten and inform the kind of religious support that so many people need. But hopefully the ways in which I use basic Quaker testimonies to build a context of communal spiritual support will suggest similar opportunities for those of you who come from other religious traditions.

Basic Quaker testimony:
There is that of God in everyone.

The deep Love in me must acknowledge the deep Love in all others, even if the other is having an experience that I do not understand or with which I do not feel comfortable.

George Fox, an early leader of the Religious Society of Friends, did not suggest that we honor "that of God in everyone unless they have out-of-the-ordinary experiences of God that make you feel uncomfortable." In fact, many of his own experiences were quite out-of-the-ordinary, both for his day and for ours.

Likewise, Jesus did not say, "Love your neighbor as yourself unless they have been labeled depressed, delusional or psychotic." Love in this context means dealing with our own fears and sending only Love to the other, while acknowledging our humanness when we do not do it perfectly. When "that of God" in one person meets "that of God" in the other, and does so in a deep place of Divine Love, then those whose personal journey touches on the mystical or on that which we do not immediately understand will feel surrounded and supported in the ways that they need.

Basic Quaker testimony:

We champion a spirit of equality.

Theoretically, we Quakers have long acknowledged people as equal, regardless of gender, race, or any other outward characteristic. But if we truly champion equality, then we must acknowledge people as equal, period. In this context, it means treating all people's experiences of God with respect, knowing that all experiences have purpose.

Some people are not less valuable humans—or more valuable—because they have or have not had certain kinds of experiences of God. Just as we were admonished to eliminate all cause for war, we need to eliminate all cause for shame and stigma.

We all have equal access to God, but that does not mean we travel the same path. Equal does not mean "the same" in this case any more than equal means "the same" when applied to race or gender issues.

And a spirit of equality can help us foster an environment in which all people's experiences with God are treated with equal respect.

Basic Quaker testimony:

We are committed to the ways of peace.

As Quakers, our peace testimony is usually applied to international affairs. But the peace to which we are committed is larger than that. Peace is a deep transformative process. Peace, when it is effective, occurs as people first make peace with themselves, then with one another.

As we make peace with ourselves and find ways to deal with our own fears, we are then able to be a member of a community that can provide containment for people having intense experiences.

Basic Quaker testimony:

The bottom line is compassion.

Nothing is more basic to the Quaker way than compassion. What does compassion mean in this context? I believe it means getting ourselves out of other people's way when they need to be with God. It means being a part of a community that can be nonjudgmental, honest in gentle ways, and respectful of the diverse paths of others. That is radical compassion, the testimony of a compassionate life.

Some of the most fundamental longings of those who shared their stories with me connect in natural ways with religious communities of any tradition. I mention them here in the hope that religious groupings of all kinds will be sensitive in meeting some of these most fundamental needs.

Fundamental longing:
Celebrating the joy
When we encounter those who are having pleasant or ecstatic experiences we can share their joy. Intense joy makes many people uncomfortable, but if we are to treasure the gifts that God puts in our midst, we need to learn to say thank-you for the joy—and celebrate its presence.

Fundamental longing:
Listening at deep spiritual levels
We need to move away from the culturally taught practice of labeling experiences of God as delusional. Instead of suppressing the content, we need to move toward deep spiritual listening with one another. It's important to listen with respect and with nonjudgment, sharing in return both one's own perspectives as well as one's own limits. Deep listening goes beyond superficial levels. As Chief Papunchang suggested in the journal of John Woolman, it means listening even to "the place where words come from."

Fundamental longing:
Containing intense energy
The need for containment emerged repeatedly in the stories that I was told. A "container" is a safe environment in which to be with the experience. For some, the energy of the opening has become too intense for them to contain without help. They may require the help of a spiritual director or a mental health professional. Sensitive and supportive religious communities can also help serve as a needed container.

Fundamental longing:
Supporting those in crisis
A person in crisis needs accompaniment and love. When the crisis

is severe, accompaniment may need to occur twenty-four hours a day until it subsides. In some places, the only resource available is a psychiatric unit of a hospital. Yet such a unit may not provide the spiritual understanding and ongoing compassion that a thoughtful religious community can provide. Sometimes the ideal context is a combination of the two.

Some of what is needed in a safe container is determined by the circumstances and particularities of any given situation. For example, abuse and trauma arose repeatedly as issues that had to be dealt with as one was opened to the mystical. Spiritual directors and religious communities are often not prepared for the intensity that can arise when individuals begin to deal with such issues. Help from professionals may be warranted.

Choosing mental health professionals who are knowledgeable of the work of the Spirit and are sympathetic is crucial. Choosing spiritual directors who know when to ask for therapeutic help is equally critical. Religious groups need to identify therapeutically knowledgeable spiritual directors as well as spiritually open therapeutic professionals in the local community before a crisis occurs so that there will be easy access and appropriate suggestions without a lot of fumbling around or inappropriate delay.

Several components of a safe container appeared in many of the stories of participants. Caring religious communities will check to see that these components are in place whenever they are providing critical support for those who are feeling a need for a safe container for intense experiences:

Critical component:
Make sure the person is taking care of basic needs.
Enough exercise, healthy food, and more water than usual are important. A person engaged in the rich inner life may have more need for sleep (or at least rest), as well as an increased need for quiet and contemplation. From those around them, the one undergoing such an experience needs respect, genuineness, gentleness, honesty, and non-judgment.

Critical component:
Help the person rely on his or her inner guide.
Most of those in extreme crisis turned their lives over to others for help because they came to a place they could not make their own decisions or direct their own lives. Most indicated that this was a last re-

sort. Individuals need to be in control of their own lives for as long as possible. To stay in control of their own lives, they must stay in a relationship of trust with their own inner guide. A safe container will facilitate for as long as possible individuals' exploration of what their own inner guide is telling them to do, rather than providing external suggestions. Helping them to hear what that inner guide is saying—and helping them trust that guide—can be most valuable.

Critical component:
Urge caution in terms of who the person talks with.

Over and over, I have heard people say that they learned to be very careful with whom they shared their experiences of God. This care is important even for the person experiencing no fear and who has very adequate frameworks for integrating their experiences in positive ways.

R.D. Laing talks about the "tyranny of the sane" in describing how repressive it can be when one tries to conform to the demands of the "sane" society. Likewise, Pseudodionysius talks about how important it is to share the mystical only with those who have been "initiated." In the Gospel of Matthew, it is suggested that we not "cast our pearls before swine."

It's not that any of us should be silent—far from it. There is much to be gained by sharing. Nevertheless, it's critical that a supportive religious community that is trying to function as a container provide people with whom individuals can safely share their precious experiences of the sacred.

Critical component:
Foster a caring conversational environment.

It's helpful if those with experiences to share are encouraged to discern before they speak. They might ask themselves, am I telling this story to someone who can honor it—and am I honoring God in the telling? Does the person to whom I will speak treat the stories of others with respect? Likewise, those who do the listening should be reminded of the importance of being respectful, honest, nonjudgmental, and genuine. A caring religious community might even make it a point to foster and practice this kind of listening and this kind of sharing, even before a safe container is needed.

Critical component:
Listen to where the words come from.

In his book *On Listening to One Another,* Douglas Steere gives many clues about good listening. One of the ones that I like best is this:

> In his journal, John Woolman tells the story of standing to pray
> in a religious meeting among the Indians living along the
> Susquehanna River. When an interpreter stood to translate
> Woolman's words into the Indian language, he was asked to sit
> down. After the meeting, Chief Papunchang said of the prayer he
> had not understood, "I love to feel where words come from."

To support others as they share personal stories of experiences of God, our listening needs to go beyond labels of "mysticism" or "mental illness." By listening to others in a way that allows us to truly feel where their words come from, we are able to accompany one another on some of the most significant journeys of our lives.

Critical component:
Provide accompaniment rather than "problem solving."
In many contexts, problem-solving is a good way of helping one another. Religious communities can swing into problem-solving mode rather easily. But it seems that when people are sharing their deepest experiences of God, problem solving is not as helpful as simple accompaniment. Accompaniment requires sitting with uncertainty without trying to fix anything. It requires that control be maintained by the one who is sharing out-of-the-ordinary experiences. For a religious community, it can be hard work, but it is valued. Participants repeatedly told me that accompaniment is what they long for.

Critical component:
Respect and acknowledge boundaries.
In building safe containers, it is important to pay attention to boundaries. In the spiritual context, we loosen boundaries to feel connected. In the mental health context, we tighten boundaries to keep out unwanted experiences and content in our lives. We all have boundaries, and each of us is unique.

When we are listeners, it is important that we listen from the frame of reference and values of the speaker. But we all have limits to what we can listen to. It is important to be clear. It is important to be able to say, for example, "I cannot be with this person or listen to this story because it hooks me and my issues, and I don't remain clear." It is important to determine what our limits are, respecting our own frame of reference and our own values. In any kind of community, it is important to be clear about where our boundaries lie.

Critical component:
Provide loving and prayerful support.

In the August 1998 issue of a newsletter called *What Canst Thou Say*, Pat McBee says that discernment of one's relationship with the Divine is a personal matter. She adds, however, that "the community plays essential roles in grounding our spiritual sensibilities and in providing direct and indirect support in the process of discernment." Possibilities for this kind of support can be found in informal conversations, spiritual friendships, support groups, spiritual direction, eldering, clearness committees, and other means. "Discernment," she writes, "can be greatly strengthened by the loving and prayerful support of other Friends."

Critical component:
Encourage integration.

Someone has said, "All love is God, and God is all love." Maybe that's why the separations that happen inside us weaken us. We are most strong when we can integrate into one coherent whole all parts of ourselves and our experiences. Religious communities that seek to function as safe containers for those whose journeys include new or unusual experiences need to look for ways to encourage the integration of those experiences into the lives of those who have experienced them.

UNDOING THE VIOLENCE
Ginny's story about the importance of integration

I believe that the separation in my life weakened me. The weakening made me vulnerable to a kind of terror. I spent many years defending against that fear. Unacknowledged fear lead me to do some really harmful things to others. The violence that I did to other people around me was more subtle and death-producing than hitting. It was the violence of hiding behind my intellect, hiding behind my degrees, hiding behind my status, hiding behind big words. I was hiding from my daily "important" work, hiding from the realization of who I am without all that "stuff."

Acting from a place of unacknowledged fear leads to violence, and sometimes it is a "sneaky violence." In this country, we keep building larger prisons and locking up more and more people in those gray cement buildings behind barbed wire. That is a sneaky violence. When I judge those more courageous than I, those who can live their feelings, even their terror, then I too am violent.

When I judge, I require a person's soul and spirit to stay locked in their skin because I make it unsafe to come out around me. That is violence of no smaller magnitude. And it's the kind of violence I engaged in when I hadn't put the parts of me back together.

The positive integration of mystical experiences into one's life is a task that will occupy much of one's energy. Perhaps that is why participants in this study have so valued the opportunity to share their experiences in faith communities and to have those experiences accepted, just as they are, without labeling or judging. This context of sharing and acceptance enables individuals to integrate their experiences in the most positive manner.

Faith communities can also encourage healthy integration by helping individuals move away from those acknowledged and unacknowledged fears that can be so destructive. When individuals, because of such fears, resist the experiences that they have been given, they are more likely to persist in destructive behaviors. Fear can distort both the experience and its importance.

Discernment also plays a role in understanding and integrating mystical experiences. Some ask how to easily discern whether what they have experienced is a "true" spiritual experience or a psychiatric problem. But as I have suggested in previous chapters, such questions contain within them assumptions that seek to impose their own reality. Discernment is necessary, but faith communities need to remember that it is important for individuals to discern their own names for their experiences and it is important for individuals to be provided with the extended time that it usually takes to determine what lies within and what lies without one's own Truth. Discernment is not snap judgment. Sometimes one must live with an experience for a while.

Over the centuries, hundreds of ways have been proposed for discerning what is of God and what is not. Sometimes discernment has been done in ways that genuinely helped a person toward a richer quality of life. Sometimes not.

In examining the history of both Christianity and Quakerism, I did not find much consistency among the many different discernment methods that have been used. But I did find a persistent connection to power. When a group or individual wants to take power from another, they typically label the other's experiences of God as false, evil, inauthentic, or heresy. Our latest Western contribution to this pattern is to call it "delusional." This kind of "discernment" functions to promote the agenda of those in power. Gender, political, and social abuses abound. An obvious example is the repression of women's spirituality during the witch-hunt era. Early Quakers likewise faced political repression when discernments of what is "truly" of God by the wider religious culture did not include the practices of Quakers. Another example is the way that the pre-Reformation patriarchal Christian church enhanced its power by telling believers that the clergy had to mediate their experiences of God.

Certain tools *have* proven helpful in the discernment process. It's true that the rigid use of even the most helpful tools can turn abusive, especially when using the language of polarities (authentic vs. inauthentic, for example). So caution is appropriate. But the baby can be thrown out with the bath water if useful tools are ignored simply because of the danger of misuse.

A helpful tool cited by many participants in this study is found in Galatians 5:22–23, which says, "The fruit of the Spirit is love, joy, peace, patience, kindness, generosity, faithfulness, gentleness, and self-control" (NRSV). Self-control is rendered as temperance in some translations. Assessing the effect of an experience on one's life is a more productive line of testing than looking at the nature of an individual experience. And such an assessment, by its very nature, must be done over a period of time.

Many other good guides for discernment in contemporary life can be found. In the February 1988 issue of *Shalem News,* for example, Gerald May reflects on "authentic spiritual experience." He obviously comes from a slightly different philosophical context than I do, but his guides for discerning "authentic" experiences can be useful as guidance tools.

His article outlines eight qualities that may help in reflecting on experiences, and I include them here (translated into language that I find more natural) because others have found them to be useful statements on which to build their own queries. I suspect that faith communities might benefit from keeping these in mind as they seek to provide safe containers for those in their midst who find themselves on mystical journeys.

Guide for discernment:
Meaningful integration
The first quality that May cites as a guide is meaningful integration. Spiritual experiences do not·exist as isolated "highs." They occur within the context of real life and are integrated in a way that is meaningful for both the individual and the community. Authentic experiences may contain a perfect end-in-itself quality, but they still have meaning and impact on life.

Guide for discernment:

The bearing of good fruit

The second quality that May mentions is bearing good fruit for both individuals and communities. Classically, this includes deepened faith, hope, trust, compassion, creativity, and love.

Guide for discernment:

Decreased self-preoccupation

Authentic experiences lead people to feel more identified with and more open to the rest of humanity and the world, rather than feelings of being more special or "better" than other people.

Guide for discernment:

Increased self-knowledge

May suggests that spiritual experiences lead to a greater understanding of oneself rather than repression, denial, or a shutting out of self-awareness.

Guide for discernment:

Humility with dignity

Fifthly, May suggests that authentic experiences of God lead to a particular kind of humility, one that painfully recognizes more of one's human inadequacy while at the same time increasingly realizes one's own preciousness and worth as a child of God. It is a humility that is combined with dignity. This is in contrast to experiences that lead either to arrogance or a devaluing of oneself.

Guide for discernment:

An openness to differences

The sixth quality mentioned by May is an openness to differences. By deepening trust in the power and goodness of God, authentic experiences lead to less defensiveness about one's own faith and increased respect for and openness to dialogue with people of differing faiths rather than a defensive or aggressive clinging to one's own understanding.

Guide for discernment:

A personal open-endedness

According to May, authentic spiritual experiences contain a quality of further invitation. There is a deepened yearning and inspired energy for continued growth and healing rather than an easy sense of "having arrived."

Guide for discernment:

An appreciation for that which is "ordinary"

Although authentic experiences may initially be accompanied by either celebration and enthusiasm on the one hand or fear and trepidation on the other, the integration of those experiences brings a quality of wondrous appreciation for that which is "ordinary." There is a recognition that life is holy, and the miraculous presence of God's grace flows through all of it. A strong separation of the holy from the mundane should be questioned.

No matter what tools and qualities one looks for, discernment during the night portion of the journey is especially difficult. When I look back on my own dark times, I can see that the lessons that I learned have become some of the most important and powerful lessons of my life. Yet those were the times that I thought I was most "crazy"—or at least felt that way. I would not seek again the experiences that I had, but I know that they were critical learning times for the calling that I am being prepared for. I can think of no other way in which I could have learned those lessons. Many participants in this project have said similar things. The task of the "dark night" is to increase faith. But in those hours before morning comes, it is indeed a hard time.

Because of this, faith communities need to remember that some of the guidelines and tools that work so well when used over time do not work so well in the midst of what some have called "the midnight hour." Many of us have to go through a period in which much destruction goes on in our lives—to make room for the new life whose seed has already been planted. There may also be times where our very survival requires a period of self-preoccupation. We may have to pay such close attention to what we ourselves need that it becomes hard to have energy for others. Such times are especially hard for those who have been "givers" all their lives. Yet there are times that even "givers" must learn to receive.

The guidelines given in Galatians and the guidelines given by Gerald May work well as long as they are used with some flexibility and are used to discern over the long-term. If we cling to them for assessment of specific moments in the journey, they can easily be misused.

St. John of the Cross says that all of our experiences must ultimately be judged on the Love that is generated over our lives. What better discernment can there be than this?

Beyond-ordinary experiences have been documented in literature as a part of human life for thousands of years. Today there are debates about the "right" words and "right" frameworks for understanding these experiences. Are these experiences gifts from God or workings of evil? Do they represent shamanic teachings or mental illness or brain chemistry? Are they some combination of things? There are many choices.

It is important for both individuals and religious communities to remember that the words, the frameworks, and the societal institutions that we use are human in origin. They are incomplete, imperfect, and do not represent whole Truth. Therefore we need to take responsibility for choosing words, frameworks, and societal institutions that enhance our lives and that enable greater Love to flow through our spirits.

It is important for each person to sort out over time what she or he believes to be of God and what is not. But while in crisis, the priority is often to assess what resources are available and how best to use them. Choices have to be made. At certain points, the critical questions become, "Which professionals will help me best deal with this situation? Should I turn to religious professionals, such as ministers or spiritual directors? Should I seek the help of mental health professionals? What role can my faith community play? Do I need a combination of resources?"

When dysfunction is a part of one's experiences, each individual must work with carefully chosen professionals to define the state of health that he or she is working towards. And religious communities need to stand ready to support and enhance such choices.

When we share stories of our mystical journeys with God and when we listen to one another in "that deep place where words come from," we give each other incredible gifts. There are gifts in the sharing for those of us who may be either religious or mental-health professionals. There are gifts in the sharing for those of us who draw our strength from our spiritual heritage or are an active part of a faith community. And there are gifts in the sharing for those of us who have experienced the mystical.

More people are beginning to talk about their experiences. And it is my hope that as time goes by, as we each glean more and more from the literature and stories that are shared, an even greater number of people will say "no" to those traditional views and methodologies that have so often pathologized both the spiritual and the person having spiritual experiences.

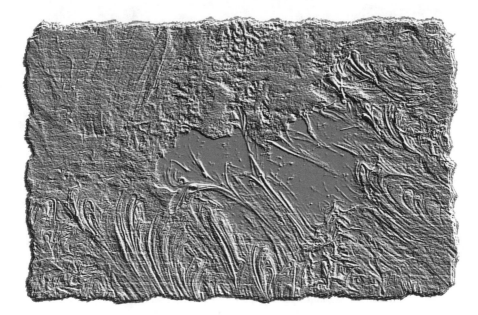

CHAPTER 14

On the Dance Floor: Loving Accompaniment

J OURNEYS ALONG mystical paths may take us to places we had not intended. We may be invited to dance to music that we don't yet know. At times, we may even resist when the Spirit invites us. Our old luggage, heavy and painful, may remain firmly clutched at our side.

But the Divine Presence is not easily refused—and does not even mind our dancing with our luggage.

The remarkable thing is that the Divine Presence keeps leading in love. We may give in only gradually at first. But with each new step, we find our values changing, our vision transformed. Something remarkable has taken hold.

Margareta McKenna understands some of this. She is a Quaker, a member of Dublin Monthly Meeting and Ireland Yearly Meeting. Her words resonate with much that I have been trying to say, and as I bring this book to a close, I want to share with you here a story that she has told.

THE DANCE HALL

An image shared by Margareta McKenna

The following vision came to me not in a dream but while I was awake. In it, I see myself in an old dance hall, of the very plain variety you would find in the Irish countryside a couple of decades ago. There is a row of chairs along one of the walls where all the women sit. The men are huddled together at the door. I sit on one of the chairs.

Surrounding me on the floor is the luggage I have picked up during my life. There are many suitcases and rucksacks and shopping bags and small handbags. They contain everything that makes up the person that is Margareta McKenna—all my memories, all that I have been taught about how to behave in this world, my thoughts on the meaning of life, my emotional memories, my fears and doubts, my ideas about God. In my vision, it is extremely important for me to hold on to my luggage. I mustn't lose it as I would then lose my identity. What would be left of me?

So I am quite happy to sit there minding my luggage. But then something unexpected happens. God comes up to me and asks me for a dance. I am, of course, flattered—and honored. But regretfully I have to decline the offer, for while I'm up on the dance floor, someone might come along and steal my luggage. I don't want that to happen.

God accepts my explanation but returns after a while with another invitation to dance. This time I reply, "Thanks very much, but you see, I'm not very good at dancing, and anyway I'm happy to sit here and watch the others dance."

Once again, God accepts my excuse, but God returns again and again and again with further invitations. In the end, I get fed up and I say, "OK God, I'll give you *one* dance."

I bend down and pick up all my suitcases and my bags. I have to bring them with me onto the dance floor, lest someone come along and steal them. But soon I understand that it is impossible to dance while carrying all that luggage, so I put them back on the floor.

I enter into the dance with the Dancing Partner who knows all there is to know about dancing and who patiently teaches me each new step. I quickly realize what a pleasure and a joy it is to trustingly allow myself to be led in the dance. I had no idea dancing would be such fun!

After a while, in my vision, I ceased to care about what happened to my luggage. For all I know, the next day, when the cleaners came to clean the dance hall, they found it where I left it and simply took it away.

Having entered the dance with the Dancing Partner and having left all that luggage behind doesn't mean, however, that I don't discover from time to time some more bags that I have been holding, unbeknownst to me. It's almost as if the Dancing Partner is lovingly and joyously leading me in the dance to places where I can see myself in a new light, places where I am presented with new callings and am again presented with new ways of letting go of that which holds me back.

I hope that this book has reminded you that the Presence is made manifest in many different ways. It is not ours to call any of God's ways "crazy."

People come to the presence of God as they are, with whatever psychological baggage they have accumulated. Even if we are not yet ready to let go of our luggage, God will still dance with us. For a time, we may try to carry all of it, even as we dance. We let go as we can.

It is ours to promote deep and compassionate spiritual listening. It is ours to learn how to build effective containers—and deeply respectful dance floors—where people can dance between love and fear, moving toward Love in relative safety, letting go of the baggage as they are ready, while freely dancing with the baggage as long as they need to.

As a dancer, I will not dance on concrete floors. They are too hard, and I risk the danger of being hurt. I will, however, dance on a floor of wood. It is organic. It has give. It moves when I move.

In like manner, I am called to a dance of loving accompaniment with sisters and brothers who are having out-of-the-ordinary experiences of God. The dance floor on which we dance is made of respect, honesty, nonjudgment, and compassion. Prayer is the name of the basic step. God is the choreographer.

I am grateful for the dance to which I have been called.

Dare I invite you to join in?

APPENDIX A:
RESOURCES

THE FOLLOWING NEWSLETTERS, tapes, and other resources may be of value to you if you would like to explore further some of the issues and themes raised in this book:

What Canst Thou Say Newsletter. c/o Carol Roth, 532 Lakeview Avenue, Pitman NJ 08071.
Center for Psychological and Spiritual Health. 1782 Church Street, San Francisco CA 94131.
Kundalini Research Network. c/o Bonnie Greenwell, PO Box 1150, Cupertino CA 95015.
Spiritual Madness: The Necessity of Meeting God in Darkness Audio Tapes. Sounds True, PO Box 8010, Boulder CO 80306.

On the other hand, if what you would like to do is to examine for yourself some of the books and articles cited or used in preparing this volume, consider the following:

American Psychiatric Association, *Diagnostic and Statistical Manual, Fourth Edition.* Washington, D.C.: American Psychiatric Association, 1994.
Geoffrey Keynes, editor, *The Complete Writings of William Blake.* London, Oxford University Press, 1966.
Howard Brinton, *Ethical Mysticism in the Society of Friends.* Wallingford, Pennsylvania: Pendle Hill Publications, 1967.
J. Campbell, *Heroes with a Thousand Faces.* New York: Viking Press, 1973.
Sandra Cronk, *Dark Night Journey.* Wallingford,

Pennsylvania: Pendle Hill Publications, 1991.

M.W. Heery, "Inner Voice Experiences: An Exploratory Study of Thirty Cases," *Journal of Transpersonal Psychology.* Volume 21, Number 1, pp. 73–82 (1989).

William James, *The Varieties of Religious Experience.* New York: Random House (1902).

A.W. Jones, *Journey into Christ.* New York: The Seabury Press, 1977.

Rufus Jones, "Mystical Religion and the Abnormal," in *New Studies in Mystical Religion.* New York: Macmillan & Company, 1927.

Rufus Jones, *Studies in Mystical Religion.* London: Macmillan & Company, 1923.

C.G. Jung, *Memories, Dreams, and Reflections.* New York: Vintage Books, 1960.

R.D. Laing, *The Divided Self.* London: Penquin Books, 1969.

D.B. Larson, E.M. Pattison, A.R. Omran, and B.H. Kaplan, "Systematic Research on Religious Varieties in Four Major Journals, 1978–1982," *American Journal of Psychiatry.* Volume 143, pp. 329–334 (1986).

M.B. Liester, "Inner Voices: Distinguishing Transcendent and Pathological Characteristics," *Journal of Transpersonal Psychology.* Volume 28, Number 1, pp. 1–29 (1996).

M.B. Liester, "A Relativity Theory of Consciousness," unpublished manuscript (1999).

R.A. Lockhart, "Mary's Dog is an Ear Mother: Listening to the Voices of Psychosis," *Psychological Perspectives.* Volume 6, Number 2, pp. 144–160 (1975).

D. Lukoff, "Transpersonal Perspectives on Manic Psychosis:

Creative, Visionary, and Mystical States," *Journal of Transpersonal Psychology.* Volume 20, Number 2, pp. 111–135 (1988).

D. Lukoff, F. Lu, and R. Turner, "Diagnosis: A Transpersonal Clinical Approach to Religious and Spiritual Problems" in *The Textbook of Transpersonal Psychiatry and Psychology,* Bruce W. Scotten, Allan B. Chinen, and John R. Battista, editors. New York: Basic Books, Harper/Collins, 1989.

D. MacDonald, L. LeClair, C. Holland, A. Alter, and H. Friedman, "A Survey of Measures of Transpersonal Constructs," *Journal of Transpersonal Psychology.* Volume 27, Number 2, pp. 171–193 (1995).

D. McClelland, *Psychoanalysis and Religious Mysticism.* Wallingford, Pennsylvania: Pendle Hill Publications, 1959.

R.W. Medlicott, "An Inquiry into the Significance of Hallucinations with Special Reference to Their Occurrence in the Sane," *International Record of Medicine and General Practice Clinics.* 171-L, pp. 664–665 (1958).

J.S. Miller, "Mental Illness and Spiritual Crisis: Implications for Psychiatric Rehabilitation," *Psychosocial Rehabilitation Journal.* Volume 14, Number 2, pp. 29–47 (1990).

B.L. Owen, *A Heuristic Study of the Experiences of the Breakthrough of the Sacred.* Dissertation: Saybrook Institute, 1995.

J.W. Perry, *The Self in Psychotic Process.* Dallas: Spring Publications, 1987.

M.C. Richards, "Wrestling with the Daimonic" in *The Crossing Point.* 1971.

J.K. Singer, *The Unholy Bible: A Psychological Interpretation of William Blake.* New York: G.P. Putnam's

Sons, 1970.

S. Stahlman, "The Relationship Between Schizophrenia and Mysticism." Essay posted on the worldwide web, 1996.

D. Steere, *On Listening to One Another.* New York: Harper & Brothers, 1955.

Evelyn Underhill, *The Essentials of Mysticism.* New York: E.P. Dutton, 1960.

R. Walsh, "Science and Religion—Proposals for Reconciliation: An Essay Review of Ken Wilber's 'The Marriage of Sense and Soul: Integrating Science and Religion," *Journal of Transpersonal Psychology.* Volume 29, Number 2, pp. 123–139 (1997).

Ken Wilber, *A Brief History of Everything.* Boston: Shambhala, 1996.

Ken Wilber, *The Eye of Spirit: An Integral Vision for a World Gone Slightly Mad.* Boston: Shambhala, 1997.

Ken Wilber, *No Boundary: Eastern and Western Approaches to Personal Growth.* Boston: Shambhala, 1979.

Ken Wilber, *Psychologia Perennis: The Spectrum of Consciousness* and *Paths Beyond Ego: The Transpersonal Vision.* Los Angeles: Jeremy P. Tarcher, 1993.

Ken Wilber, *The Spectrum of Consciousness.* Wheaton, Illinois: Qwest, 1993.

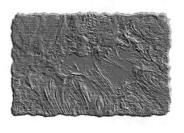

APPENDIX B:
QUESTIONNAIRE

THE FOLLOWING QUESTIONNAIRE was used to elicit initial information from most of the participants in this study. In most cases, the questionnaire was followed up with personal conversation and interaction.

Mysticism Research Questionnaire

Name _____

Physical Address _____

Email Address _____

Phone _____

Religious Affiliation _____

If Quaker, Monthly Meeting _____

　　　　　　　 Yearly Meeting _____

Gender _____

Age _____

Education (highest level completed) _____

Occupation _____

Please attach separate sheets as needed to answer the following questions:

1.　　　What is your definition of mysticism?

2.　　　Have you had experiences that you would label as religious mystical experiences? What were they? Could you talk about them with others? Did you ever feel like you were "going crazy"? Were you fearful? If yes, what might have helped to lessen the fear? With whom could you talk about your experiences? With whom could you not talk about them? When you talked about them, how were you received? What was helpful in the responses of others? What was not helpful? Do you call yourself a mystic? Why or why not?

3.   Have you had psychic experiences or those involving extrasensory perception? Do you believe this kind of experience is part of mystical experience? Are they the same? Are they different? How?

4.   Have you or do you know anyone that has been formally labeled with a category of mental illness because of "religious delusions" or other religious experiences? What was that like?

5.   How have these experiences been integrated into your life in positive ways? In negative ways? What were the factors that contributed to the integration process in positive and negative ways? How have these experiences transformed your life and your understanding of the purpose of your life?

6.   Have you heard others describe their religious mystical experiences? Do you respond to some with more openness than others? What makes you more open to some than to others? What internal "tests" are you using—cues to you that this is OK or cues to you that is not for you?

7.   What questions would you like to have answered on this topic? What would you like to read about after I have done this research? What ideas do you have for this research?

ABOUT THE AUTHOR

Jennifer Elam

JENNIFER ELAM is a licensed psychologist who has studied, practiced, and taught psychology since 1969. For most of her career, she taught at the college level, worked in residential treatment, and worked in schools with students aged preschool through adult.

In 1996 Jennifer took a four-year leave of absence from her psychology work. She became a student of Quakerism, mysticism, and art at Pendle Hill, a Quaker center for study and contemplation. During the 1997–1998 resident student year at Pendle Hill, Jennifer was a Cadbury scholar. She listened to many people's stories of their experiences of God and recorded about one hundred of them, many of which came to influence the paintings that she was creating. This book grew out of the work that she did to integrate her career in psychology with her spiritual life.

Jennifer presently leads art retreats, facilitates programs at the Listening Center in Springfield, Pennsylvania, works as a psychologist, and makes time to write and paint. Her heart's desire now is to enjoy ordinary life.